Spending the Night with Lorne Michaels

Dana Rasmussen

The role of the book within our culture is changing. The change is brought on by new ways to acquire & use content, the rapid dissemination of information and real-time peer collaboration on a global scale. Despite these changes one thing is clear--"the book" in it's traditional form continues to play an important role in learning and communication. The book you are holding in your hands utilizes the unique characteristics of the Internet -- relying on web infrastructure and collaborative tools to share and use resources in keeping with the characteristics of the medium (user-created, defying control, etc.)--while maintaining all the convenience and utility of a real book.

Contents

Articles

Mr. Saturday Night — 1
Lorne Michaels — 1

Lorne's Early Days — 7
Rowan & Martin's Laugh-In — 7

Live from New York, It's Saturday Night — 26
Saturday Night Live — 26

Lorne's Production Company — 43
Broadway Video — 43

Great Comedies Produced by Lorne — 49
Three Amigos — 49
Coneheads (film) — 52
Wayne's World (film) — 56
Tommy Boy — 62
Brain Candy — 66
A Night at the Roxbury — 71
Mean Girls — 75
Baby Mama (film) — 83
MacGruber (film) — 87

A Select Few TV Comedies Produced by Lorne — 92
The Hart and Lorne Terrific Hour — 92
Sunday Night — 93

References

Article Sources and Contributors 116

Image Sources, Licenses and Contributors 117

Mr. Saturday Night

Lorne Michaels

Lorne Michaels	
Michaels at the 2010 Time 100 Gala.	
Birth name	Lorne David Lipowitz
Born	November 17, 1944 Toronto, Ontario, Canada
Medium	film, television
Nationality	Canadian, American
Years active	1968 – present
Spouse	Rosie Shuster (1973 – 1980) (divorced) Susan Forristal (1981 – 1987) (divorced) Alice Barry (1991 – present) 3 children
Notable works and roles	*Saturday Night Live* (1975–present)
Website	Official website [1]
Emmy Awards	

> **Outstanding Comedy Series**
> 2007 *30 Rock*
> 2008 *30 Rock*
> 2009 *30 Rock*
> **Outstanding Variety, Music or Comedy Series**
> 1976 *Saturday Night Live*
> 1977 *Saturday Night Live*
> 1993 *Saturday Night Live*
> **Outstanding Variety, Music or Comedy Special**
> 1999 *Saturday Night Live: 25th Anniversary*
> **Outstanding Writing for a Variety, Music or Comedy Program**
> 1978 *Saturday Night Live*
> 1989 *Saturday Night Live*
> 2002 *Saturday Night Live*
> **Outstanding Writing in a Variety, Music or Comedy Special**
> 1973 *Lily (1973 special)*
> 1975 *The Lily Tomlin Special*
> 1977 *The Paul Simon Special*

Lorne Michaels, CM (born November 17, 1944) is a Canadian television producer, writer and comedian best known for creating and producing *Saturday Night Live* and producing the various film and TV projects that spun off from it.

Early life

Michaels was born **Lorne David Lipowitz** in Toronto, Ontario, Canada, the son of Florence (née Becker) and Henry Abraham Lipowitz, a furrier. He was the eldest of the Lipowitz children. He has a sister, Barbara Lipowitz, who currently resides in Toronto and a brother, Mark Lipowitz, who died from a brain tumor. Michaels attended the Forest Hill Collegiate Institute in Toronto and graduated from University College, University of Toronto, where he majored in English, in 1966. Michaels began his career as a writer and broadcaster for CBC Radio. He moved to Los Angeles from Toronto in 1968 to work as a writer for *Laugh-In* and *The Beautiful Phyllis Diller Show*. During the late 1960s, Michaels married Rosie Shuster, who later worked with him on *Saturday Night Live* as a writer. She was the daughter of Frank Shuster, one half of the famous comedy team, Wayne and Shuster. Michaels and Shuster were divorced in 1980.

Saturday Night Live

In 1975, Michaels created (with fellow NBC employee Dick Ebersol and president of the network Herb Schlosser) the TV show *NBC's Saturday Night*, which in 1977 changed its name to *Saturday Night Live*. The show, which is performed live in front of a studio audience, immediately established a reputation for being cutting edge and unpredictable. It became a vehicle for launching the careers of some of the most successful comedians in the world.

Originally the producer of the show, Michaels was also a writer and later became executive producer. He occasionally appears on-screen as well, where he is known for his deadpan humor. Throughout the show's history, *SNL* has been nominated for more than 80 Emmy Awards and has won 18. It has consistently been one of the highest-rated late-night television programs. Michaels has been with *SNL* for all seasons except for his hiatus in the early 1980s (seasons 6–10).

His daughter Sophie has appeared in episodes, one of which was during the show's 30th season hosted by Johnny Knoxville during the monologue when Lorne introduces Johnny Knoxville to his daughter and Sophie shocks Knoxville with a taser. She also appeared in a sketch about underage drinking when Zac Efron hosted the show.

Perhaps Michaels's best-known appearance occurred in the first season when he offered the Beatles $3000 - a deliberately paltry sum - to reunite on the show. He later upped his offer to $3200, but the money was never claimed. According to an interview in Playboy magazine, John Lennon and Paul McCartney happened to be in New York City that night and saw the show. They very nearly went, but changed their minds as it was getting too late to get to the show on time, and they were both tired. This near-reunion was the basis for the TV movie *Two of Us*.

He has had combative relationships with several cast members, and is generally portrayed by media onlookers as a harsh but effective boss. One source of conflict is his rather active disdain of improvisation during the performances of SNL, despite the extensive background and training in improvisational comedy many of SNL's performers have had.

Other work

Michaels started Broadway Video in 1979, producing such shows as *The Kids in the Hall*.

During his *SNL* hiatus, Michaels created another sketch show entitled *The New Show*, which debuted on Friday nights in prime time on NBC in January 1984. The show failed to garner the same enthusiasm as SNL.

In the 1980s, Michaels appeared in an HBO mockumentary titled *The Canadian Conspiracy* about the supposed subversion of the United States by Canadian-born media personalities, with Lorne Greene as the leader of the conspiracy. Michaels was identified as the anointed successor to Greene.

Michaels is also an Executive Producer of *Late Night* on NBC and also works as executive producer of the NBC show *30 Rock*.

Honors

In 1999, Michaels was inducted into the *Television Academy Hall of Fame*. In 2002, Michaels was made a member of the *Order of Canada* for lifetime achievement, and awarded a star on the *Hollywood Walk of Fame*.

In 2003, he received a star on Canada's Walk of Fame.

In 2004, he was awarded the Mark Twain Prize for American Humor by the John F. Kennedy Center for the Performing Arts. Speaking at the awards ceremony, original *Saturday Night Live* cast member Dan Aykroyd described Michaels as "the primary satirical voice of the country."

In Canada, Michaels also received a 2006 Governor General's Award for Lifetime Artistic Achievement.

In 2008, Michaels was awarded the Webby for Film & Video Lifetime Achievement. With the allotted 5-words allowed to each recipient, his five word acceptance speech was "Five words is not enough."

In popular culture

Dr. Evil, a character of Mike Myers's in the Austin Powers films, has been rumored to be partly based on Michaels. Myers has denied the rumors, saying that the two share only a voice.

Mark McKinney of the comedy team, *The Kids in the Hall* has stated that his character, Don Roritor, the president of Roritor Pharmaceuticals in the film *Brain Candy*, is based on Lorne Michaels.

Michaels was played by Ari Cohen in the 2002 TV movie *Gilda Radner: It's Always Something*.

Michaels has been mentioned on three episodes of *The Simpsons* (every time as the butt of jokes).

Michaels at the 2008 Tribeca Film Festival.

In a 2008 interview with *Playboy*, Tina Fey admitted that Alec Baldwin's character Jack Donaghy on *30 Rock* is inspired by Michaels. In a different interview, Baldwin stated some of his inspiration for Donaghy was drawn from Michaels.

Personal life

Michaels became a U.S. citizen in 1987. He has two sons, Henry and Edward, one of whom attends Dartmouth College as a member of the Class of 2014, and a daughter, Sophie (who cameoed on the season 30 episode of *SNL* hosted by Johnny Knoxville in the monologue where the cast and crew members perform *Jackass* stunts on Knoxville). He has been married three times, first to *SNL* writer Rosie Shuster (1967; div. 1980), then to model Susan Forristal (1984; div. 1987), and currently to his former assistant Alice Barry (1991 to present). Lorne has given money to the campaigns of Senators Barack Obama, Chris Dodd and John McCain over the years.

Filmography

As producer, except as noted

- *Gilda Live* (1980) (writer and producer)
- *Nothing Lasts Forever* (1984)
- *Three Amigos* (1986)
- *Wayne's World* (1992)
- *Coneheads* (1993)
- *Wayne's World 2* (1993)
- *Lassie* (1994)
- *Tommy Boy* (1995)
- *Stuart Saves His Family* (1995)
- *Black Sheep* (1996)
- *Kids in the Hall: Brain Candy* (1996)
- *A Night at the Roxbury* (1998)
- *Superstar* (1999)
- *Man on the Moon* (1999) (appearing as self, uncredited)
- *The Ladies Man* (2000)
- *Enigma* (2001)
- *Mean Girls* (2004)
- *Hot Rod* (2007)
- *Baby Mama* (2008)
- *MacGruber* (2010)

Selected television credits

- *The Hart and Lorne Terrific Hour* (1970–71) (costar, writer, producer)
- *Saturday Night Live* (1975–1980; 1985–present) (executive producer, creator)
- *All You Need Is Cash* (aka *"The Rutles"*) (1978) (executive producer)
- *Mr. Mike's Mondo Video* (1979) (executive producer)
- *The New Show* (1984) (producer)
- *Sunday Night* (1988–1990) (executive producer)
- *The Kids in the Hall* (1989) (executive producer)
- *Late Night with Conan O'Brien* (1993-2009) (executive producer)
- *The Rutles 2: Can't Buy Me Lunch* (2002) (executive producer)
- *The Colin Quinn Show* (2002) (executive producer)
- *Sons and Daughters* (2006) (producer)
- *30 Rock (2006-present) (executive producer)*
- *Late Night with Jimmy Fallon (2009-Present) (executive producer)*

References

External links

- Official website [1]
- Lorne Michaels [1] on National Public Radio in 2005
- The Museum of Broadcast Communications - *Encyclopedia of Television* "Saturday Night Live" [2]
- Lorne Michaels [3] at the Internet Movie Database
- Lorne Michaels [4] at the Internet Broadway Database

Lorne's Early Days

Rowan & Martin's Laugh-In

Rowan & Martin's Laugh-In	
Caricatures of Dan Rowan and Dick Martin by Sam Berman	
Also known as	*Laugh-In*
Genre	Sketch comedy
Created by	Ed Friendly George Schlatter
Directed by	Gordon Wiles Mark Warren
Starring	Dan Rowan Dick Martin Gary Owens Goldie Hawn Ruth Buzzi Henry Gibson Arte Johnson Alan Sues Jo Anne Worley Lily Tomlin Judy Carne
Country of origin	United States
No. of seasons	6
No. of episodes	140 (List of episodes)
Production	
Running time	45–48 minutes
Broadcast	
Original channel	NBC
Original run	January 22, 1968 – March 12, 1973
Status	Ended
Chronology	

Preceded by	Pilot (September 9, 1967)
Followed by	*Laugh-In's 25th Anniversary* (February 7, 1993) *Rowan & Martin's Laugh-In Christmas Present* (December 2, 1993) *Rowan & Martin's Laugh-In: A Valentine's Day Special* (February 14, 1994)
Related shows	*Turn-On*

Rowan & Martin's Laugh-In is an American sketch comedy television program which ran for 140 episodes from January 22, 1968, to May 14, 1973. It was hosted by comedians Dan Rowan and Dick Martin and was broadcast over NBC. It originally aired as a one-time special on September 9, 1967 and was such a success that it was brought back as a series, replacing *The Man from U.N.C.L.E.* on Mondays at 8 pm (EST).

The title, *Laugh-In,* came out of events of the 1960s hippie culture, such as "love-ins" or "be-ins." These were terms that were, in turn, derived from "sit-ins", common in protests associated with civil rights and anti-war demonstrations of the time.

The show was characterized by a rapid-fire series of gags and sketches, many of which conveyed sexual innuendo or were politically charged. The co-hosts continued the exasperated straight man (Rowan) and "dumb" guy (Martin) act which they had established as nightclub comics. This was a continuation of the "dumb Dora" acts of vaudeville, best popularized by Burns and Allen. Rowan and Martin had a similar tag line, "Say goodnight, Dick".

Laugh-In had its roots in the humor of vaudeville and burlesque, but its most direct influences were from the comedy of Olsen and Johnson (specifically, their free-form Broadway revue *Hellzapoppin'*), the innovative television works of Ernie Kovacs, and the topical satire of *That Was The Week That Was*.

A typical episode's format

- Shortly after the beginning of the show, after a minute or two of Rowan/Martin standup, Rowan would intone: "C'mon Dick, let's go to the party". This live-to-tape segment comprised all cast members and occasional surprise celebrities dancing before a 1960s "Mod" party backdrop, delivering one- and two-line jokes interspersed with a few bars of dance music (later adopted on *The Muppet Show*, which had a recurring segment that is similar to "The Cocktail Party" with absurd moments from characters).
- "The Mod, Mod World" segment, with its own signature tune, comprised brief sketches on a theme interspersed with film footage of female cast members go-go dancing in bikinis, their bodies painted with punchy phrases and pithy wordplay. The dancers were usually Goldie Hawn, Judy Carne and Chelsea Brown; Ruth Buzzi and Jo Anne Worley popped up rarely, as did frequent guest Pamela Austin. In the 1969/1970 season, the chore was handled briefly by new cast members Teresa Graves and Pamela Rodgers before the go-go dancing became the domain of uncredited extras.)

- The Farkel Family, a couple with *many* kids —all of whom had flaming red hair and freckles like neighbor Ferd Berfel (played by Dick Martin). Head of the family Frank Farkel never questioned this fact when Ferd visited. Most plots were excuses to force the cast into alliterative tongue-twisters ("That's a fine-looking Farkel flinger you found there, Frank"). Bespectacled baby daughter Flicker Farkel (played by Buzzi) had no lines except screaming "Hiiii!!!" Two of the kids were twins named Simon and Gar Farkel (played by cast members of different races; originally Goldie Hawn and Chelsea Brown, later Pamela Rodgers and Teresa Graves).
- "Laugh-In Looks at the News", a parody of network news, introduced by an unjournalistic song and dance chorus line including the female cast members, and often a female guest celebrity (or on one occasion, Don Rickles in a tutu). This commented on current events. The segment often included "News of the Past" which lampooned historical events, and "News of the Future", predicting unlikely or bizarre future stories to comic effect. Rowan actually nailed some, mentioning "President Ronald Reagan" in a story from "1988, 20 years from now", eliciting laughter. Another prediction, that the Berlin Wall would be destroyed in 1989, also came true, although the follow-up gag that it would be "quickly replaced by a moat full of alligators" obviously did not. The news segment was reminiscent of BBC's earlier *That Was the Week That Was* and in turn, was echoed a few years later by *Saturday Night Live's* "Weekend Update" segments. *Saturday Night Live* creator Lorne Michaels was a Laugh-In writer early in his career.
- New Talent Time, introducing oddball variety acts. The most famous of these performers was Tiny Tim. Comedian Paul Gilbert, father of actress Melissa Gilbert, appeared as inept "French" juggler "Paul Gilbert" (pronounced "jheel-bare" in the French manner). Comic Art Metrano appeared as "The Great Metrano," a so-called magician who had no skill at all. *Laugh-In* writer Chris Bearde liked the "New Talent" concept and later developed it into *The Gong Show*.
- The Flying Fickle Finger of Fate Award, saluting actual dubious achievements by the government or famous people, such as the announcement of a new Veterans Administration hospital to be erected in Southern California shortly after another such facility was destroyed in the Sylmar earthquake of 1971. The trophy was a gilt, outstretched finger atop a square base. "The flying, fickle finger of fate" was already a familiar catchphrase on the show (Dan Rowan would use the phrase when ushering "new talent" like Tiny Tim on stage).
- Judy Carne was often tricked into saying "Sock it to me", which led to her being doused with water or otherwise assaulted. ("It may be rice wine to you, but it's still sake to me!")
- At the end of every show, Dan Rowan turned to his co-host and said, "Say good night, Dick", to which Martin replied, "Good night, Dick!" (varying a bit from the old George Burns and Gracie Allen radio show). The show then featured cast members opening panels in a psychedelically painted 'joke wall' and telling jokes. As the show drew to a close and the applause died, executive producer George Schlatter's solitary clapping continued even as the screen turned blank and the production logo, network chimes, and NBC logo appeared.

Memorable cast members/guests and their running gags

- Arte Johnson portrayed a number of recurring characters, including:
  - **Wolfgang the German soldier** – Wolfgang would comment on the previous gag by saying "Verrry interesting", sometimes with comments such as "...but *shtupid*!" He eventually would close each show by talking to Lucille Ball as well as the cast of *Gunsmoke* — both airing opposite *Laugh-In* on CBS; as well as whatever was on ABC. Johnson would later repeat the line while playing Nazi-themed supervillain Virman Vundabar on an episode of *Justice League Unlimited*.
  - **Tyrone F. Horneigh** (pronounced "hor-NIGH," presumably to satisfy the censors) – A dirty old man coming on to Gladys Ormphby (Ruth Buzzi) seated on a park bench, who almost invariably clobbered him with her purse. Sample exchange:

    Tyrone: Do you believe in the hereafter?

    Gladys: Of course I do!

    Tyrone: Good. Then you know what I'm *here* after!

    - (Both the Tyrone and Gladys characters went into animated form in the "Nitwits" segments of the 1977 animated television show "Baggy Pants and the Nitwits")
  - **Piotr Rosmenko**, the Eastern European Man – Piotr stood stiffly and nervously in an ill-fitting suit while commenting on differences between America and "the old country," such as "Here in America, is very good, everyone watch television. In old country, television watches you!" This predated a similar schtick by Yakov Smirnoff. Occasionally guest star Sammy Davis, Jr. teamed with Johnson as "The Rosmenko Twins."
  - **Rabbi Shankar** (a pun on Ravi Shankar), an Indian guru – Dressed in a Nehru jacket dispensing pseudo-mystical Eastern wisdom laden with bad puns. He held up two fingers in a peace sign whenever he spoke.
  - An unnamed **man in a yellow raincoat** and hat, riding a tricycle. The image of him pedaling, then tipping over and falling, was frequently used between sketches. (Judy Carne was once reported to have said that every member of the cast took turns riding the tricycle at one time or another.)
- Announcer Gary Owens standing in an old-time radio studio with his hand cupped over his ear, making announcements, often with little relation to the rest of the show, such as (in an overly-dramatic voice), "Earlier that evening..."
- Ruth Buzzi in many roles, including:
  - **Gladys Ormphby** – A drab, though relatively young spinster who was the eternal target of Arte Johnson's Tyrone; when Johnson left the series, Gladys retreated into recurring daydreams, often involving marriages to historical figures, including Christopher Columbus and Benjamin Franklin (both played by Alan Sues). She would typically hit people repeatedly with her purse.

- **Doris Swizzle** – A seedy barfly paired with her husband, Leonard Swizzle, played by Dick Martin.
- **Busy Buzzi** – A Hedda Hopper/Louella Parsons-style gossip columnist.

Ruth Buzzi would resurrect Gladys Ormphby, along with Arte Johnson's Tyrone, (their voices at least) in the animated series, Baggy Pants and the Nitwits, and she would later bring Gladys with her when she worked on Sesame Street. Buzzi also performed as Gladys on The Dean Martin Show, most notably in the Celebrity Roasts.

- Henry Gibson as:
  - **The Poet** – The Poet would hold an oversized flower and read offbeat poems. He pronounced his name "Henrik Ibsen".
  - **The Parson** – A character who made ecclesiastical quips and, in 1970, officiated at a near-marriage for Tyrone and Gladys.
- Lily Tomlin as:
  - **Ernestine/Miss Tomlin** – The obnoxious telephone operator with no concern for her customers ("'Fair'? Sir, we don't have to be fair. We're the phone company.").
  - **Edith Ann** – A child who frequently said, "And that's the truth", followed by "Pbbbt!" . Tomlin performed her skits in an oversized rocking chair that made her appear small.
  - "Tasteful" society matron **Mrs. Earbore**. Mrs. Earbore would express quiet disapproval about a tasteless joke or remark, and then rise from her chair with her legs spread, and sometimes got doused with a bucket of water.

Lily Tomlin later performed Ernestine for *Saturday Night Live* and *Happy New Year, America* (hosting the latter in character), and Edith Ann on children's shows such as *Sesame Street*.

- Judy Carne in two robotic speech and movement roles:
  - **Mrs. Robot** in "Robot Theater" – The female companion to Arte Johnson's "Mr. Robot", both equally inept
  - The talking **Judy Doll**, usually played with Arte Johnson who never heeded her warning: "Touch my little body, and I hit!"
- Henny Youngman telling one-liner jokes for no reason. Often, corny one-liners would be followed by the line, "Oh, *that* Henny Youngman!"
- Alan Sues as **Big Al** – A clueless and fey sports anchor who loved ringing his bell, which he called his "tinkle", and as hungover children's show host "Uncle Al, The Kiddies' Pal"
- Goldie Hawn was the giggling dumb blonde stumbling over her lines, especially when she introduced Dan's "News of the Future".
- Jo Anne Worley sometimes sang off-the-wall songs using her loud operatic voice, but is better remembered for her mock outrage at "chicken jokes" and her melodic outcry of "Bo-ring!". Many times, during the Cocktail Parties, she talked about her boyfriend Boris (a married man).

- Barbara Sharma as the dancing meter-maid who ticketed anything from trees to baby carriages, and often praised vice president Spiro Agnew, calling him 'Pres-ee-dent Agnew.'
- Flip Wilson, whose character, the female **Geraldine**, originated the phrase "What you see is what you get". Another catchphrase was "The devil made me do it". Wilson and his alter ego had their own variety show in the early '70s.
- Dan Rowan as **General Bull Right** – A far-right-wing representative of the military establishment and outlet for political humor.
- Richard Dawson as **Hawkins the Butler** – Would always start his piece by asking "Permission to...?" and proceed to fall over.
- **The Judge**. Originally portrayed by British comic Roddy Maude-Roxby as a stuffy magistrate with black robe and powdered wig. Each "Judge" sketch would feature an unfortunate defendant brought before the court. Guest star Flip Wilson introduced the sketch with "Here come de judge!," the venerable catchphrase of black nightclub comedian Pigmeat Markham. Markham was surprised that his trademark had been appropriated, and he petitioned producer George Schlatter to let him play The Judge himself. Schlatter complied and Markham sat atop the bench for one season. The sketches were briefly retired until another guest star, Sammy Davis, Jr., donned the judicial robe and wig. Davis immediately made The Judge his own, using a drawling dialect reminiscent of "Kingfish" Tim Moore, and enthusiastically playing every courtroom scene broadly. Davis even introduced his own sketches, strutting across a bare stage in Judge regalia and chanting in couplets ("If your lawyer's sleepin', better give him a nudge! Everybody look alive, 'cause here come de judge! Here come de judge!" – followed by a cutaway of the entire cast announcing "Order in the courtroom – here come de judge!").

Memorable moments and catchphrases

The show gave publicity to singer Tiny Tim, a large man with long dark hair, a prominent nose and a cheap suit. He sang in falsetto while accompanying himself on ukulele. Tiny Tim was Herbert Khaury, a serious scholar of Tin Pan Alley tunes who hit upon this strangely humorous characterization. Thanks to appearances on the show, he recorded a piercing version of the 1920s song "Tiptoe Through the Tulips" which became a Top-40 hit. Tiny Tim was later married on *The Tonight Show Starring Johnny Carson* to Victoria Budinger, who was known as Miss Vicki. Martin would often refer to Tim's appearances by asking Rowan with some concern, "You're not gonna bring back Tiny Tim, are you?"

During the September 16, 1968 episode, Richard Nixon, running for president, appeared for a few seconds with a disbelieving vocal inflection, asking "Sock it to *me*?" Nixon was not doused or assaulted. An invitation was extended to Nixon's opponent, Vice-President Hubert Humphrey, but he declined. According to George Schlatter, the show's creator, "Humphrey later said that not doing it may have cost him the election", and "[Nixon] said the rest of his life that appearing on *Laugh-In* is what got him elected. And I believe that. And I've had to live with that."

Other musical moments came in the first season with some of the first music videos seen on network TV, with cast members appearing in films set to the music of The Nitty Gritty Dirt Band, The Bee Gees, The Temptations, the Strawberry Alarm Clock and The First Edition.

Lily Tomlin and Goldie Hawn later became noted film stars (Hawn won an Academy Award while still a member of the cast; Tomlin was later nominated for a Best Supporting Actress Oscar in 1975 for *Nashville*). Henry Gibson later co-starred in the Robert Altman film *Nashville* and was nominated for a Golden Globe. Ruth Buzzi became a regular on children's television series. Dave Madden, whose trademark was to throw confetti (representing an unspoken impure thought) while keeping a dour expression at the punchline of a joke, played Reuben Kincaid on the television sitcom *The Partridge Family*. Richard Dawson, who previously had a regular supporting role on the sitcom *Hogan's Heroes*, went on to success on the game shows *Match Game* and *Family Feud*. Larry Hovis, also a regular on *Hogan's Heroes*, appeared on *Laugh-In* during the first and the fifth seasons. Teresa Graves parlayed her season on the show into the title role of the police drama *Get Christie Love!* Flip Wilson took Geraldine and his other characters to his own variety show from 1970 through 1974.

In addition to those mentioned, the show created numerous catchphrases:

- "Verrry eeen-ter-es-ting!" (said by Arte Johnson as Nazi soldier Wolfgang spying from behind a potted plant)
- A six-note pattern preceding a code-word or punchline to an off-color joke, such as "do-doo-doo-da-do-doo ... smack!" or "... family jewels!" (sometimes extended to 18 notes by repeating the GGGDEC pattern two more times before the code-word). This same musical phrase had been used as a "signature" at the end of many pieces played by Spike Jones and his City Slickers.
- "I didn't know that." (Dick Martin's occasional response to what happened on an episode)
- "Easy for you to say!' (Dan Rowan's reply whenever Dick Martin tripped on his tongue during a joke)
- "Ohhh, I'll drink to that." (Martin's response to something Rowan said that he liked.)
- "I was wondering if you'd mind if I said something my aunt once said to me." A phrase that Dick Martin would always say to interrupt Dan Rowan's announcements on what would happen during their next show; this phrase was followed by a story about a bizarre situation that his aunt went through.
- "Look *that* up in your *Funk and Wagnalls*! (a lesser-known set of reference books whose phonetically funny name helped the show poke fun at network censors)
- "Go to your room."
- "Uncle Al had to take a lot of medicine last night" (line by Uncle Al, the Kiddies' Pal, played by Alan Sues)
- "You bet your sweet bippy!"

- "Here come de' judge!" (reprising comedian Pigmeat Markham and further popularized by guest stars Flip Wilson and especially Sammy Davis Jr.)
- "'Ello, 'ello! NBC, beautiful downtown Burbank" (the response to calls received by a switchboard operator played by Judy Carne). When the series was syndicated in 1983, the NBC logo and the network's name were edited out.
- "And that's the truth." (Edith Ann, summarizing whatever she just said, and capping it with a juicy razzberry)
- "One ringy-dingy...two ringy-dingies..." (Ernestine's mimicking of the rings while she was waiting for someone to pick up the receiver on the other end of the telephone lines)
- "A gracious good afternoon. This is Miss Tomlin of the telephone company. Have I reached the party to whom I am speaking?" Ernestine's greeting to people whom she would call
- "I just wanna swing!" Gladys Ormphby's catchphrase
- "Is that a chicken joke?" Jo Anne Worley's outraged cry, a takeoff on Polish jokes
- "Here comes the big finish, folk!" (usually before the last of a series of a star's bad puns)
- "Sock it to me!" experienced its greatest exposure on *Laugh-In* although the phrase had been featured in songs like Aretha Franklin's 1967 "Respect" and Mitch Ryder's 1966 "Sock It To Me, Baby!"
- "Oh, *that* Henny Youngman"
- "Marshall McLuhan...what're you doin'?" (Henry Gibson)
- "I don't know. I've never been out with one!" (First introduced by guest star Marcel Marceau, this catch-all punchline would be uttered by any guest star. Goldie: "Are you of the opposite sex?" Tiny Tim: "I don't know, Miss Goldie, I've never been out with one.")
- "Blow in my ear and I'll follow you anywhere."
- "Now, that's a no-no!"
- "Tune in next week when Henny Youngman's wife burns Jell-o!"
- "If [so-and-so] married [what's-his-name], divorced him and married {etc.}" The purpose being to try to set up a tongue-twister, involving the last names of celebrities. Example: "If Rosemary Clooney married Regis Toomey. divorced him and married Mickey Rooney, divorced him and married Paul Muni, divorced him and re-married Regis Toomey, she'd be Rosemary Clooney Toomey Rooney Muni Toomey!" Sometimes, the punchline results would be take-offs of songs or plays or products: "If Kaye Ballard married former astronaut Wally Schirra, divorced him, married his brother, she'd be [*singing "Que Sera, Sera"*] Kaye Schirra Schirra."
- "Morgul the Friendly Drelb" (a pink Abominable Snowman-like character that appeared in the first episode and bombed so badly that his name was used in various announcements by Gary Owens for the rest of the series (usually at the end of the opening cast list, right after Owens himself: "Yours truly, Gary Owens, and Morgul as the Friendly Drelb!") and credited as the author of a paperback collection of the show's sketches)
- "That's the most beautiful thing I ever heard."

- "Ring my chimes!"
- "Want a Walnetto?", was a pick-up line Tyrone would try on Gladys, which always resulted in a purse drubbing.
- "We have to stop meeting like this. My wife's getting suspicious." (or some other variant form of the phrase)

Merchandise tie-ins and spin-offs

A humor magazine tie-in, *Laugh-In Magazine*, was published for two years, and a syndicated newspaper comic strip was drawn by Roy Doty and eventually collected for a paperback reprint.

The *Laugh-In* trading cards from Topps had a variety of items, such as a card with a caricature of Jo Anne Worley with a large open mouth. With a die-cut hole, the card became interactive; a finger could be inserted through the hole to simulate Worley's tongue. Little doors opened on Joke Wall cards to display punchlines.

On *Letters to Laugh-In*, a short-lived spin-off daytime show hosted by Gary Owens, cast members read jokes sent in by viewers.

The comedy film *The Maltese Bippy* featured several actors from the series.

The General Motors Corporation produced a specially modified Pontiac GTO called "The Judge" to capitalize on the phrase's popularity. "The Judge" was available in 1969, 1970 and 1971.

In 1969, Sears, Roebuck and Company produced a 15-minute short, *Freeze-In*, which starred series regulars Judy Carne and Arte Johnson. Made to capitalize on the popularity of the series, the short was made for Sears salesmen to introduce the new Kenmore freezer campaign. A dancing, bikini-clad Carne provided the opening titles with tattoos on her body (ala Goldie Hawn).

Between 2003 and 2004, Rhino Entertainment released two *Best Of* releases of the show, each containing six episodes. Unlike other shows released back in those years, the DVDs are still in print.

Cast comings and goings

Ruth Buzzi, Judy Carne, Henry Gibson, Larry Hovis, Arte Johnson and Jo Anne Worley were originally in the pilot special from 1967. Gary Owens (announcer), Eileen Brennan, Roddy Maude-Roxby, and Goldie Hawn came on in the show. Most of the cast members weren't in all 14 episodes from the season. Only the two hosts, announcer, and Judy, Henry, and Arte were in all 14 episodes. Eileen only appears in half of the episodes. She, Larry, and Roddy left after the first season.

The second season saw a handful of new people, including Alan Sues, Dave Madden, and Chelsea Brown. All of the new cast members from the second season left, except Alan Sues who stayed on until 1972.

The show was #1 in the ratings for the 1968–69 and 1969–70 seasons. At the end of '68–69, Judy Carne chose not to renew her contract, though she did make appearances during '69–70; producer George Schlatter blamed her for breaking up the "family." The show also survived the departures of Goldie Hawn and Jo Anne Worley to remain a top-20 show in '70–71. Schlatter tried to replace Hawn with other wide-eyed starlets acting dumb: first Pamela Rodgers, then Sarah Kennedy, and finally Donna Jean Young, but Hawn's dizzy characterization proved inimitable.

The third season saw several new people who only stayed on for that season, Teresa Graves, Jeremy Lloyd, Pamela Rodgers, and Stu Gilliam. Lily Tomlin joined in the middle of the season. Jo Anne Worley, Goldie Hawn, and Judy Carne left after the season.

New faces in the 1970–71 season included tall, sad-eyed Dennis Allen, who alternately played quietly zany characters and straight man for anybody's jokes; comic actress Ann Elder, who also contributed to scripts, tap dancer Barbara Sharma, who would later appear on *Rhoda*, and beefy Johnny Brown, who played the superintendent Nathan "Buffalo Butt" Bookman on *Good Times*.

Arte Johnson, who created many characters, insisted on star billing, apart from the rest of the cast. The producer mollified him, but had announcer Gary Owens read Johnson's credit as a separate sentence: "Starring Dan Rowan and Dick Martin! And Arte Johnson! With Ruth Buzzi..." This maneuver gave Johnson star billing, but made it sound like he was still part of the ensemble cast. Johnson left the show after the 1970–71 season. NBC aired the pilot for his situation comedy *Call Holme*, but it never became a series.

Henry Gibson also departed after the 1970–71 season. He and Johnson were replaced by Richard Dawson and Larry Hovis, both of whom had appeared occasionally in the first season. Both of them were on Hogan's Heroes. However, the loss of Johnson's many characters caused ratings to drop farther.

The show celebrated its 100th episode during the '71–72 season, and Carne, Worley, Johnson, Gibson, Graves, and Tiny Tim all returned for the festivities. John Wayne was also on hand for his first cameo appearance since 1968.

For the show's final season (1972–73), Rowan and Martin assumed the executive producer roles from George Schlatter (known on-air as "CFG", which stood for "Crazy Fucking George") and Ed Friendly.

Except for holdovers Dawson, Owens, Buzzi, and only occasional appearances from Tomlin, a new cast was brought in. This final season featured future *Match Game* panelist Patti Deutsch, folksy singer-comedian Jud Strunk, and ventriloquist act Willie Tyler and Lester. Deutsch, Strunk, and Tyler caught on to the spirit of the show and made valuable contributions (Deutsch did celebrity impressions—in the presence of the celebrity—and took over Worley's role in "The Farkel Family"). The shows were still amusing, but without the usual gang, viewers didn't respond as they once had.

These last shows never aired in the edited half-hour rerun syndicated (through Lorimar Productions) to local stations in 1983 and later aired on Nick at Nite. The cable network Trio started airing the show in its original one-hour form in the early 2000s, but only the pilot and the first 69 episodes (extending to the fourth episode of the 1970–71 season) were included in Trio's package. Two "Best-of" DVD packages are also available; they only contain six episodes each.

Of over three dozen entertainers to grace the cast, only Rowan, Martin, Owens and Buzzi were there from beginning to end. Owens wasn't in the 1967 pilot and Buzzi missed two first-season episodes.

Ratings

- 1968–1969: #1
- 1969–1970: #1
- 1970–1971: #13
- 1971–1972: #22

Revival

In 1977, Schlatter and NBC briefly revived the property as a series of specials – entitled simply *Laugh-In* – with a new cast, including former child evangelist Marjoe Gortner. The standout was a then-unknown Robin Williams, whose starring role on ABC's *Mork & Mindy* one year later prompted NBC to rerun the specials as a summer series in 1979. Rowan and Martin, who owned part of the *Laugh-In* franchise, were not involved in this project. They sued Schlatter for using the format without their permission, and won a judgment of $4.6 million in 1980.

Regular performers (with season numbers, where known)

- All seasons: Dan Rowan, host
- All seasons: Dick Martin, host
- All seasons: Gary Owens, announcer
- All seasons: Ruth Buzzi
- Season 1: Eileen Brennan (1968)
- Season 1, 2, 3: Judy Carne (1968–1970)
- Season 1, 2, 3, 4: Henry Gibson (1968–1971)
- Season 1, 2, 3: Goldie Hawn (1968–1970)
- Season 1, 5: Larry Hovis (1968, 1971–1972)
- Season 1, 2, 3, 4: Arte Johnson (1968–1971)
- Season 1: Roddy Maude-Roxby (1968)
- Season 1, 2, 3: Jo Anne Worley (1968–1970)
- Season 2, 3, 4, 5: Alan Sues (1968–1972)
- Season 2: "The Fun Couple" Charlie Brill and Mitzi McCall (1968–1969)
- Season 2: Chelsea Brown (1968–1969)

- Season 2: Dave Madden (1968–1969)
- Season 2: Pigmeat Markham (1968–1969)
- Season 2: Dick "Sweet Brother" Whittington (actor/disc jockey) (1968–1969)
- Season 2, 3: Byron Gilliam (1969–1970; uncredited in season 2, returned as dancer only in 5)
- Season 3: Teresa Graves (1969–1970)
- Season 3: Jeremy Lloyd (1969–1970)
- Season 3: Pamela Rodgers (1969–1970)
- Season 3: Stu Gilliam (1970)
- Season 3, 4, 5, 6: Lily Tomlin (1969–1973)
- Season 3, 4, 5 Johnny Brown (1970–1972)
- Season 4, 5: Dennis Allen (1970–1973)
- Season 4, 5: Ann Elder (1970–1972)
- Season 4: Nancie Phillips (1970–1971)
- Season 4, 5: Barbara Sharma (1970–1972)
- Season 4: Harvey Jason (1970–1971)
- Season 4, 5, 6: Richard Dawson (1971–1973; also one appearance in Season 1)
- Season 6: Moosie Drier (1971–1973)
- Season 6: Tod Bass (1972–1973)
- Season 6: Brian Bressler (1972–1973)
- Season 6: Patti Deutsch (1972–1973)
- Season 6: Lisa Farringer (1972–1973)
- Season 6: Sarah Kennedy (1972–1973)
- Season 6: Jud Strunk (1972–1973)
- Season 6: Willie Tyler (1972–1973)
- Season 6: Donna Jean Young (1972–1973)

Regular guest performers

- Jack Benny (1968–1970, 1972)
- Johnny Carson (1968–1970, 1971, 1973)
- Sammy Davis Jr. (1968–1970, 1971, 1973)
- Zsa Zsa Gabor (1968–1970)
- Peter Lawford (1968–1971)
- Tiny Tim (1968–1970, 1971–1972)
- John Wayne (1968, 1971–1973)
- Flip Wilson (1968–1970)
- Henny Youngman (1968–1969, 1971–1973)

Full list of celebrity guest performers

1968

- Leo G. Carroll
- Barbara Feldon
- Lorne Greene
- Buddy Hackett
- Sheldon Leonard
- Strawberry Alarm Clock
- Robert Culp
- Kenny Rogers & The First Edition
- Tom Smothers
- Tim Conway
- Sonny & Cher
- Paul Gilbert
- Don Adams
- The Nitty Gritty Dirt Band
- Douglas Fairbanks Jr.
- Walter Slezak
- Kaye Ballard
- Richard Dawson
- Dinah Shore
- The Temptations
- Jerry Lewis
- Leonard Nimoy
- Edward Platt
- Connie Stevens
- Larry Storch
- Paul Williams
- Sally Field
- Terry-Thomas
- Joby Baker
- Godfrey Cambridge
- Anissa Jones
- Pat Morita
- Paul Winchell
- Elgin Baylor
- Harry Belafonte

- Joey Bishop
- Regis Philbin
- The Bee Gees
- Ed McMahon
- John Byner
- Hugh Downs
- James Garner
- Shelley Berman
- Milton Berle
- Jill St. John
- Hugh Hefner
- Bob Hope
- Jack Lemmon
- Richard Nixon
- Sonny Tufts
- Herb Alpert
- Eve Arden
- Arlene Dahl
- George Kirby
- Patrick Wayne
- Nick Castle
- Greer Garson
- Abbe Lane
- Greg Morris
- Otto Preminger
- Michael Wayne
- Kirk Douglas
- Lena Horne
- Liberace
- France Nuyen
- Bobby Darin
- Rosemary Clooney
- Mitzi Gaynor
- The Holy Modal Rounders
- Colonel Sanders
- Van Johnson
- Werner Klemperer
- Bill Dana

- Jimmy Dean
- Marcel Marceau
- George Gobel
- Dick Gregory
- Rock Hudson
- Rod Serling
- Victor Borge
- Phil Harris
- Perry Como
- Joseph Cotten
- Phyllis Diller
- Vincent Price
- Tony Curtis
- Cliff Robertson
- Barbara Bain
- Billy Barty
- Martin Landau
- Guy Lombardo
- Nanette Fabray
- George Jessel
- Bob Newhart
- Rich Little
- Kate Smith

1969

- Peter Falk
- Marcel Marceau
- Garry Moore
- Paul Winchell
- Perry Como
- David Janssen
- Van Johnson
- George Gobel
- Guy Lombardo
- Richard and Pat Nixon
- Nancy Sinatra
- The Smothers Brothers
- Tony Curtis
- Frank Gorshin

Rowan & Martin's Laugh-In

- George Jessel
- Janos Prohaska
- Tom Kennedy
- Liberace
- Rich Little
- Don Rickles
- Cliff Robertson
- Greer Garson
- The Monkees (w/o Peter Tork)
- Nipsey Russell
- Robert Wagner
- James Drury
- James Garner
- Gina Lollobrigida
- Doug McClure
- Mel Brooks
- Lena Horne
- Rock Hudson
- Bob Newhart
- Connie Stevens
- Ann Miller
- Shelley Winters
- Forrest Tucker
- Werner Klemperer
- Laurence Harvey
- Billy Graham
- Debbie Reynolds
- Peter Sellers
- Michael Caine
- Bob Hope
- Sonny & Cher
- Mitzi Gaynor
- Jack E. Leonard
- Lana Wood
- Anne Jackson
- Romy Schneider
- Eli Wallach
- Buddy Hackett

- Carol Channing
- Diana Ross
- Tennessee Ernie Ford
- Sid Caesar
- Engelbert Humperdinck
- Jill St. John
- Roger Moore
- Jacqueline Susann
- Lorne Greene
- Ed McMahon
- Frank Sinatra, Jr.

Series writers

George Schlatter, Lorne Michaels, Phil Hahn, Jim Mulligan, Jack Hanrahan, Gene Farmer, Jim Abell, Bill Richmond, Don Reo, Allan Katz, Jack Wohl, Larry Siegel, John Rappaport, Allan Manings, Jack Margolis, Bob Howard, John Jay Carsey, Richard Goren (also credited as Rowby Greeber and Rowby Goren), Chris Bearde (credited as Chris Beard), Chet Dowling, David Panich, Marc London, Paul Keyes, Dave Cox, Jack Kaplan, Stephen Spears, Hugh Wedlock Jr., Coslough Johnson (Arte Johnson's twin brother), Hart Pomerantz, Barry Took, Digby Wolfe, Jeremy Lloyd.

Musical direction and production numbers

The musical director for *Laugh-In* was composer-lyricist Billy Barnes, who wrote all of the original musical production numbers in the show. Barnes is the creator of the famous Billy Barnes Revues of the 1950s and 1960s, and composed such popular hits as "(Have I Stayed) Too Long at the Fair" recorded by Barbra Streisand and the jazz standard "Something Cool" recorded by June Christy.

Episodes

Main article: List of Rowan & Martin's Laugh-In episodes

Production technique

The show was pre-recorded at NBC's Burbank Facility. Since timecode-controlled videotape editing had not been invented at the time, montage was achieved by the error-prone method of physical splicing of the two-inch quadraplex tape. This had the incidental benefit of ensuring that the master tape would be preserved, since a spliced tape could not be recycled for further use. *Laugh-In* Editor Arthur Schneider won an Emmy Award in 1968 for his pioneering use of the "jump cut" – the unique editing style in which a sudden cut from one shot to another was made without a fade-out.

Shows similar to *Laugh-In*

- NBC's *Laugh-In* inspired CBS's *Hee Haw*, which debuted in 1969.
- ABC's *Turn-On* is perhaps the most infamous imitator of Laugh-In. Produced by Friendly and Schlatter, *Turn-On* was even faster paced and more raunchy than *Laugh-In*, to the point where ABC cancelled the series after only one episode (in fact, some stations pulled it from the air halfway through).
- The animated show, Groovie Goolies, was influenced by *Laugh-In*, most notably in their version of the Joke Wall called *"Weird Window Time"* in which the denizens of Horrible Hall, would tell jokes and one liners from various windows, doors, etc.
- *You Can't Do That On Television* was heavily influenced by *Laugh-In* for having the use of slime poured on people's heads when they say "I don't know" (like "sock it to me" on Laugh-In) as well as using school lockers as a device similar to Laugh-In's joke wall. Ruth Buzzi was also a regular on its short-lived prime-time spinoff, *Whatever Turns You On* (which in itself is one of the many recurring comedy taglines of Laugh-In fame).
- In one episode of *Here Come the Double Deckers*, *Man's Best Friend*, they put on a show which is clearly a spoof of *Laugh-In*.

Awards and nominations

TV Land Awards

- Nominated: Favorite Variety Show (2003)

Logie Award

- Won: Best Overseas Show (1969)

Golden Globe Award

- Won: Best Supporting Actress – Television, Ruth Buzzi (1973)
- Nominated: Best Supporting Actress – Television, Lily Tomlin (1972)
- Nominated: Best Supporting Actor – Television, Henry Gibson (1971)
- Nominated: Best TV Show – Musical/Comedy (1970)
- Won: Best TV Show (1969)
- Nominated: Best TV Show (1968)

Emmy Awards

- Nominated: Outstanding Achievement by a Performer in Music or Variety, Ruth Buzzi (1972)
- Nominated: Outstanding Achievement by a Performer in Music or Variety, Lily Tomlin (1972)
- Won: Outstanding Directorial Achievement in Variety or Music, Mark Warren (For episode #4.7, 1971)
- Nominated: Special Classification of Outstanding Program and Individual Achievement – Individuals, Goldie Hawn (1970)
- Won: Special Classification Achievements – Individuals (Variety Performances), Arte Johnson (1969)
- Nominated: Special Classification Achievements – Individuals (Variety Performances), Ruth Buzzi (1969)
- Nominated: Special Classification Achievements – Individuals (Variety Performances), Goldie Hawn (1969)
- Won: Outstanding Musical or Variety Program, George Shlatter (For the September 9, 1967 special, 1968)
- Won: Outstanding Musical or Variety Series, George Shlatter (1968)
- Won: Outstanding Writing Achievement in Music or Variety, Chris Bearde, Phil Hahn, Jack Hanrahan, Coslough Johnson, Paul Keyes, Marc London, Allan Manings, David Panich, Hugh Wedlock, Jr., Digby Wolfe (1968)

See also

- Turn-On

External links

- *Rowan & Martin's Laugh-In.com* [1]
- *Rowan & Martin's Laugh-In* [2] at the Internet Movie Database
- WFMU Article on the Laugh-In writers relationship with Richard Nixon [3]
- FBI review of an episode devoted to the agency, quoted by *Harper's Magazine* in 2006 [4]

Live from New York, It's Saturday Night

Saturday Night Live

Saturday Night Live	
The *Saturday Night Live* inter-title season 35.	
Also known as	*NBC's Saturday Night* (1975–1977) *Saturday Night Live '80* (1980)
Format	Stand-up comedy, Sketch comedy, Comedy, Variety
Created by	Lorne Michaels
Directed by	Dave Wilson (1975–1986, 1989–1995) Paul Miller (1986–1989) Beth McCarthy-Miller (1995–2006) Don Roy King (2006–present)
Starring	See Saturday Night Live cast
Narrated by	Don Pardo (1975–1981, 1982–present) Bill Hanrahan (1981) Mel Brandt (1981–1982)
Country of origin	United States
Language(s)	English
No. of seasons	36
No. of episodes	683 (as of October 9, 2010) (List of episodes)
Production	
Executive producer(s)	Lorne Michaels (1975–1980, 1985–present) Jean Doumanian (1980–1981) Dick Ebersol (1981–1985)
Location(s)	Studio 8H, GE Building, Rockefeller Center, New York City, New York, United States
Running time	90 minutes (including commercials)

Production company(s)	Broadway Video
	SNL Studios
Broadcast	
Original channel	NBC
Picture format	480i (SDTV)
	1080i (HDTV)
Original run	October 11, 1975 – present
Chronology	
Related shows	*TV Funhouse*
	Saturday Night Live Weekend Update Thursday
External links	
Official website [1]	

Saturday Night Live (***SNL***) is a live late-night television sketch comedy and variety show developed by Lorne Michaels and Dick Ebersol. It premiered on NBC, a terrestrial television network in the United States, on October 11, 1975, under the title *NBC's Saturday Night*.

The show's sketches often parody contemporary Culture of the United States and politics. *Saturday Night Live* features a two-tiered cast consisting of repertory members, also called the "Not Ready For Prime Time Players" (the name used by the show's original cast), and newer cast members who are known as "Featured Players."

Each week, the show features a host who delivers an opening monologue and performs in sketches with the cast. A musical guest also performs. With the exception of season 7, the show has begun with a cold open sketch that ends with someone breaking character and proclaiming, "Live from New York, it's Saturday Night!"

For all but five seasons (six through ten), the show has been overseen by its creator and current executive producer, Lorne Michaels. Broadway Video, SNL Studios, and NBC jointly manage production. *Saturday Night Live* is one of the longest-running network television programs in the United States with nearly 700 episodes broadcast over the span of 36 seasons as of 2010. A number of the show's sketches have been developed into feature films.

Throughout its three decades on air, *Saturday Night Live* has received a number of awards, including 21 Primetime Emmy Awards, a Peabody Award, and three Writers Guild of America Awards. In 2000, it was inducted into the National Association of Broadcasters Hall of Fame. It was ranked tenth on *TV Guide*'s "50 Greatest TV Shows of All Time" list, and in 2007 it was listed as one of *Time* magazine's "100 Best TV Shows of All-*TIME*." In 2009, it received 13 Emmy nominations giving it a total of 126, giving it the most Emmy nominations in television history.

History

History of *Saturday Night Live* series:

1975–1980
1980–1985
1985–1990
1990–1995
1995–2000
2000–2005
2005–2010
Weekend Update

See also: history of SNL *by season*: 1, 2, 3, 4, 5, 6, 7, 8, 9, 10, 11, 12, 13, 14, 15, 16, 17, 18, 19, 20, 21, 22, 23, 24, 25, 26, 27, 28, 29, 30, 31, 32, 33, 34, 35, 36

In the early 1970s, NBC ran *The Best of Carson* reruns of *The Tonight Show* that aired on either Saturday or Sunday night, at an affiliate's discretion, from January 1965 until September 1975 (originally known as *The Saturday/Sunday Tonight Show Starring Johnny Carson*). In 1974, Johnny Carson wanted the weekend shows to be pulled and aired during the week. Carson wanted to save them for when he took time off.

NBC approached Dick Ebersol in 1974 and asked him to create a show to fill the Saturday night timeslot. Ebersol then approached Lorne Michaels, wanting to create a variety show that would push the boundaries with its edgy style of humor. Ebersol knew Michaels was capable of creating a show since he had worked on *Rowan & Martin's Laugh-In*. The show was set, and Michaels searched for people to join the staff. He hired Dan Aykroyd, John Belushi, Chevy Chase, George Coe, Jane Curtin, Garrett Morris, Laraine Newman, Michael O'Donoghue, and Gilda Radner to the cast. Originally, the show was called *NBC's Saturday Night*, as the current title was in use by rival network ABC. NBC purchased the rights to the name in 1976 and officially adopted the new title on March 26, 1977.

The show was an instant hit following its debut, and as a result, the cast members became suddenly famous. Chase left the show during the second season and was replaced by a new and upcoming comic named Bill Murray. Aykroyd and Belushi left the show after season four. The following season, Michaels chose to leave the show and explore other avenues. Michaels' departure led most of the cast and writing staff to leave the show as well.

Although *SNL* was still popular, Michaels thought NBC would cancel the show upon his departure. However, NBC had already planned to replace him with Jean Doumanian. NBC wanted to build up a new cast and continue on with the show, leaving Doumanian with full creative control. After disastrous reviews and behind-the-scenes turmoil, Doumanian was fired after one season. She was replaced by Dick Ebersol, who had originally hired Michaels to create the show.

Ebersol fired most of the people Doumanian hired except for a few people including unknown comics Eddie Murphy and Joe Piscopo. Ebersol remained with the show until 1984. In the fall of 1984, Ebersol departed from tradition by adding several cast members with established comedic careers, including Billy Crystal, Martin Short, and Harry Shearer. After that season, Ebersol wanted a more significant revamp, including departing from the show's established "live" format. Ebersol left the show and Michaels decided to return to the show.

Michaels returned to the show for the 1985–86 season. The entire cast from the previous season did not return, causing Michaels to rebuild the show. He hired then unknowns Joan Cusack, Robert Downey, Jr. and many others. The season was disastrous, and the show was almost cancelled. However, Michaels was given one more chance to save the show. He fired most of the staff and brought in a new set of people he hoped would save the show including Dana Carvey, Nora Dunn, Phil Hartman, Jan Hooks, Victoria Jackson, Jon Lovitz, Dennis Miller and Kevin Nealon.

Creator Lorne Michaels in April 2008.

After a slow start, the show was saved as a result of high ratings and improved critical reception. Michaels' return restored an association with NBC that has lasted nearly 30 years. As head of Broadway Video and SNL Studios, Michaels has profited from the talent he's helped introduce, producing the TV series *Late Night* (during the eras of Conan O'Brien and Jimmy Fallon - both *SNL* alumni) and *30 Rock* (a comedy created by former *SNL* head writer Tina Fey, and loosely based on her experiences in that role). Michaels also produced the TV film *All You Need Is Cash*, and a lengthy list of feature films based on *SNL* sketches; the most commercially and critically successful of these was *Wayne's World*.

Production

Cast

Main article: Saturday Night Live cast

The cast, known on-air as "The Not Ready For Prime-Time Players" at the show's beginning (a term which is still often used unofficially, and originally devised as a takeoff of the "Prime Time Players" moniker for the cast of the ABC show), is currently divided into two tiers: the more established group of repertory players; and newer, unproven cast members known as featured players, who may eventually "graduate" to the regular cast laminate. The show's current cast is listed below:

Repertory players
- Fred Armisen (2002–present)
- Abby Elliott (2008–present)
- Bill Hader (2005–present)
- **Seth Meyers** (2001–present)
- Bobby Moynihan (2008–present)
- Andy Samberg (2005–present)
- Jason Sudeikis (2005–present)
- Kenan Thompson (2003–present)
- Kristen Wiig (2005–present)

Featured players
- Vanessa Bayer (2010–present)
- Paul Brittain (2010–present)
- Taran Killam (2010–present)
- Nasim Pedrad (2009–present)
- Jay Pharoah (2010–present)

bold denotes Weekend Update anchor only

Writers

Main article: List of Saturday Night Live writers

Announcer

Don Pardo served as the announcer for the series when it first began, and has performed as the show's announcer for all seasons except for season 7, when Mel Brandt and Bill Hanrahan filled that role. Pardo, who was 57 when the show debuted, and who retired from NBC in 2004, at age 92 still flies in from his home in Tucson, Arizona, to introduce the show.

He announced that for the 36th season, he would pre-record his parts from his home in Arizona rather than performing live in New York City.

The *SNL* Band

Main article: Saturday Night Live Band

The Saturday Night Live Band (also known as "The Live Band") is the house band for *SNL*. Academy Award-winning composer Howard Shore served as the first musical director, from 1975 to 1980, appearing in many musical sketches, including Howard Shore and His All-Nurse Band and (backing a U. S. Coast Guard chorus) Howard Shore and the Shore Patrol. Over the years, the band has featured several New York studio musicians including Paul Shaffer (1975–1980), Lou Marini (1975–1983), David Sanborn (1975), Michael Brecker (1949-2007), Ray Chew (1980–1983), Alan Rubin (1975–1983), Georg Wadenius (1979–1985), Steve Ferrone (1985), David Johansen (performing as Buster Poindexter), Tom Malone (who took over as musical director from 1981–1985), and G. E. Smith (musical director from 1985–1995). The band is currently under the leadership of Tower of Power alumnus Lenny Pickett and keyboardists Leon Pendarvis and Katreese Barnes. The number of musicians has varied over the years, but the basic instrumentation has been three saxophones, one trombone, one trumpet, and a rhythm section featuring two keyboards, a guitar, bass, drums, and an extra percussionist, not a permanent part of the band until Valerie Naranjo's arrival in 1995. The

1983–1984 and 1984–1985 seasons featured the smallest band, a six-piece combo. The band plays instrumentals leading in and out of station breaks; affiliates who run no advertising during these interludes hear the band play complete songs behind a "Saturday Night Live" bumper graphic until the program resumes.

Hosts/musical guests

Main article: List of Saturday Night Live guests

A typical episode of *SNL* will feature a single host, who delivers the opening monologue and performs in sketches with the cast, and a single musical guest, who will perform two or occasionally three musical numbers. In some cases, the musical guest will also be the host and fill both duties. George Carlin was first to host the show; Candice Bergen was the first female to host the show a few weeks later and again hosted only six weeks after that. Guests that have hosted five or more times are sometimes referred to as belonging to the Five-Timers Club, a term that originated on a sketch performed on Tom Hanks' fifth episode.

Production facilities

Studio

GE Building (30 Rockefeller Plaza, or "30 Rock") where the show is filmed

Since the show's inception, *SNL* has aired from Studio 8H, located on floors 8 and 9 of GE Building (30 Rockefeller Plaza, or "30 Rock"). Due to the studio originally being a radio soundstage for Arturo Toscanini and his NBC Symphony Orchestra, the layout of the studio floor and the audience positioning causes some audience members to have an obstructed view of many of the sketches. According to NBC, the 8H studio has almost perfect acoustics. The offices of *SNL* writers, producers, and other staff can be found on the 17th floor of "30 Rock."

During the summer 2005 shooting hiatus, crews began renovations on Studio 8H. With its thirty-first season premiere in October 2005, the show began broadcasting in high-definition television, appearing letterboxed on conventional television screens. Though the show is still produced in widescreen, beginning in 2008, many non-HD viewers again began seeing the show in a 4:3 aspect ratio as a side effect to the Digital television transition.

Three of the first four shows of the 1976–77 season were shot at the former NBC Studios in Brooklyn, due to NBC News using Studio 8H for Presidential election coverage.

Post-production

With onsite facilities housed on floors 8 and 17 of Rockefeller Plaza, post-production duties on live broadcasts of *Saturday Night Live* include the mixing of audio and video elements by the Senior Audio Mixer, coupled with additional audio feeds consisting of music, sound effects, music scoring and pre-recorded voiceovers. All sources are stored digitally, with shows captured and segregated into individual elements to reorganise for future repeats and syndication. The production tracking system was migrated from primarily analogue to digital in 1998, with live shows typically requiring 1.5 Terabytes of storage, consisting of audio elements and 5 cameras worth of visual elements. Elements of *Saturday Night Live* that are pre-recorded, such as certain commercial parodies, SNL Digital Shorts, and show graphics are processed off-site in the post-production facilities of Broadway Video.

Filming and photography

Studio 8H production facilities are maintained by NBC Production Services. Video camera equipment includes four Sony BVP-700 CCD cameras, and two Sony BVP-750 CCD handheld cameras, both using Vinten pedestals. A GVG 4000-3 digital component production switcher, and GVG 7000 digital component routing switcher are used to route visual feeds to the control room, with multiple digital and analogue video recorders used to store footage. Graphics are provided by a Chyron Infinit! character generator and a Quantel PictureBox. Audio facilities consist of a Calrec T Series digitally controlled analogue mixing console, and a Yamaha digital mixing console used for tape playback support and utility audio work.

As of the 35th season, the opening title sequence and opening montage of *Saturday Night Live* is shot using Canon EOS 5D Mark II and Canon EOS 7D digital SLR cameras. Typical elements are recorded at 30 fps, with slow-motion sequences shot at 60 fps, both in full 1080p high definition.

Production process

The following is a summary of the process used to produce the show. It is based in part on interviews with former *SNL* head writer and performer Tina Fey in 2000 and 2004.

Monday:
- The day begins with a topical meeting, identifying the biggest story for the show's opening.
- This is followed by a free-form pitch meeting with Lorne Michaels and the show's host(s) for the week. The official name is "The Host Meeting" but all the writers and cast members call it "The Pitch Meeting"
- Throughout the week the host(s) has much influence on which sketches get aired.

Tuesday:
- Between 9:00 p.m. Tuesday night and 7:00 a.m. Wednesday morning, anywhere from 40 to 50 scripts are written, most of which will not be broadcast.
- Once a writer's scripts are complete, he or she will often help other writers on their scripts.
- Meanwhile, Lorne Michaels has another "Pitch Meeting" with the musical guest(s) and discusses which of their current songs, two to three, they should play in the show for their music act.

Wednesday:
- All scripts get a read-through from the cast, writers, producers, Lorne Michaels and the week's host(s). Read-through is usually held in the afternoon and lasts about two and a half to three hours.
- After the read-through, the head writer(s) and the producers meet with the host(s) to decide which sketches to work on for the rest of the week, with Lorne Michaels and the host(s) having the final say.

Thursday:

- The surviving sketches are reviewed, word-by-word, by the writing staff as a whole or in two groups in the case of co-head writers.
- Some sketches which survived the cut because of their premise, but are in need of work, are rewritten completely. Others are changed in smaller ways.
- The *Weekend Update* crew starts coming together, starting with the news items written by writers dedicated all week to the segment.
- The crew comes in for rehearsal, and the music act is rehearsed as well as some of the larger, more important sketches.
- The host(s) and musical guest(s) and usually some cast members shoot two to four promos to play for NBC.

Friday:

- The show is blocked.
- The writer of each sketch acts as producer, working with the show's set designers and costumers.
- Special music is recorded for the show.

Saturday:

- The *Saturday Night Live* Band does a mid-morning rehearsal.
- At 1 p.m., with the show still far from completed, the day begins with a run-through, with props, in front of Lorne Michaels.
- This is followed by a dress rehearsal performed in front of the studio audience, which lasts from 8 p.m. - 10 p.m. (or sometimes later) and contains approximately twenty minutes of material which will be deleted from the final broadcast.

SNL's main stage, seen during rehearsals

- Lorne Michaels uses firsthand observation of the audience reaction during the dress rehearsal and input from the host(s) and head writer to determine the final round of changes, re-ordering sketches as necessary.
- Following dress rehearsal, Lorne has a meeting with the writers to discuss the final changes and gives notes about changes that could be made for the live show. The cast is updated about sketches cut after dress rehearsal and final rundown of sketches for live show on bulletin board outside of Lorne Michaels' office.
- The show then begins at 11:29:30 p.m. Eastern Time Zone.
- After the show comes the after-party which is located at various "hot-spots" in New York. Everyone involved in the show, including the host and musical guest(s), is invited.

The status of the show during the week is maintained on a bulletin board. Sketches and other segments are given labels which are put on index cards and put on the board in order of their performances. The order is based on content as well as production limitations such as camera placement and performer availability. Segments which have been cut are kept to the side of the board. As the broadcast approaches, often the writer or producer discovers the fate of his or her segment only by consulting the bulletin board.

A *60 Minutes* report taped in October 2004 depicted the intense writing frenzy that goes on during the week leading up to a show, with crowded meetings and long hours. The report particularly noted the involvement of the guest host(s) in developing and selecting the sketches in which they will appear. Similarly, there has been an A&E episode of *Biography* which covered the production process, as well as an episode of *TV Tales* in 2002 on E!.

Broadcast

Live

The show usually begins at 11:29:30 p.m. Eastern Time, unless a delay occurs. The show broadcasts for one and a half hours, ending at 1 a.m.. For the Mountain and Pacific time zones, NBC airs the prerecorded live show usually unedited, mistakes notwithstanding.

Delays

- The show was forced by the network to run on a five-second delay on three separate occasions when Richard Pryor, Sam Kinison, and Andrew Dice Clay each hosted.
- The episode scheduled for October 25, 1986, hosted by Rosanna Arquette, was not aired until November 8 due to NBC broadcasting Game 6 of the 1986 World Series; the game entered extra innings, causing that night's broadcast of *SNL* to be cancelled. The show was recorded for the studio audience starting at 1:30 a.m. Eastern Time, and broadcast two weeks later with an "apology" by New York Mets pitcher Ron Darling.
- The episode scheduled for February 10, 2001, hosted by Jennifer Lopez, aired 45 minutes late due to an XFL game. Lopez and the cast were not told they were airing on a delay.
- During Eddie Murphy's last season, he negotiated to record a number of extra sketches in September 1983 that featured him and were broadcast in episodes for which he was not available. His last live show was with host Edwin Newman on February 25, 1984.
- The January 9, 2010, show hosted by Charles Barkley was delayed for 36 minutes when NBC's coverage of an NFL WildCard playoff game between the Philadelphia Eagles and the Dallas Cowboys ran late.

Reruns

SNL reruns are aired out of its original broadcast sequence, usually determined by which episodes have not yet been repeated, but had high ratings or acclaim for its live broadcast. Shows usually air twice during a particular season, but often the highest-rated shows of the season have a second encore show toward the end of the off-season, or episodes will be repeated a second or third time to coincide with a new event connected with the person who hosted. For example, the Natalie Portman episode aired in March 2006 to promote *V for Vendetta* was repeated August 5, 2006, before the film's DVD release August 8. Similarly, Jeff Gordon's episode reran following NBC's coverage of the Pepsi 400.

NBC and Broadway Video both hold the underlying rights, while the copyright to every episode of the show made thus far lies solely with NBC. From 1990 until 2004, Comedy Central and its predecessor Ha! re-aired reruns of the series, after which E! Entertainment Television signed a deal to reruns. Abbreviated thirty and sixty minute versions of the first five seasons aired as *The Best of Saturday Night Live* in syndication beginning in the 1980s and later on Nick at Nite in 1988, VH1, Comedy Central and E! Entertainment Television.

Compilations

From time-to-time, *SNL* airs compilation shows. Such shows will feature selected sketches from the previous season; of a particular cast member or multiple-time host; or centered on a particular theme (e.g., Halloween, Christmas). Political sketches are typically culled for a special in presidential election years; the 2000 special was notable for having self-deprecating (though separate) appearances by candidates George W. Bush and Al Gore. During the 2008 presidential race, Hillary Rodham Clinton, Mike Huckabee, John McCain, Barack Obama, Rudy Giuliani, and Sarah Palin all made appearances on the show.

Replaced/altered sketches

Encore showings are not always identical to the original broadcast.

Successful sketches aired later in the show during the original broadcast may be reedited to appear earlier. In the earlier years of the show's history, reruns occasionally replaced weaker sketches with segments from other episodes, usually from episodes that did not have an encore showing at all.

Controversial acts by a host or musical guest can be altered or removed.

- A portion of Martin Lawrence's 1994 monologue concerning feminine hygiene has been removed from all repeats, replaced with a voice-over and intertitles stating that the excised portion "...was a frank and lively presentation, and nearly cost us all our jobs."
- Sinéad O'Connor's October 3, 1992 live performance, during which she tore up a photograph of Pope John Paul II, was replaced with the dress rehearsal performance from earlier that evening where she holds up a picture of a starving African child.

- When Sam Kinison delivered a comic monologue in 1986, NBC removed his plea for the legalization of marijuana from the West Coast broadcast and all subsequent airings.

Occasionally, sketches originally performed in the dress rehearsal (which is recorded as a backup) have replaced the live version in reruns. due to errors (either technical or by the actors) in the live broadcast. Examples include:

- In 2009, during the season premiere, Jenny Slate was in a "Biker Babe" sketch where she, co-star Kristen Wiig and host Megan Fox used the word "frickin'" repeatedly. Slate accidentally slipped and said "fuckin'" instead, which was later overdubbed with "frickin'" for subsequent repeats.
- A Peter Sarsgaard sketch from his January 21, 2006 appearance, involving Rachel Dratch's fake newscast, met with technical difficulties during the live broadcast when the in-sketch TV stopped working and a stagehand was seen fixing it.
- A sketch involving "butt pregnancy" during the first broadcast of the November 12, 2005 Jason Lee episode was replaced with a musical sketch about cafeteria food during the repeat.
- A Debbie Downer sketch featuring Ben Affleck was pulled from later rebroadcasts and replaced with the dress rehearsal version. In this case, the replacement is referenced by a title card, explaining that the dress version "worked better".
- In 1980, Paul Shaffer became the first person to say "fucking" on the show. *SNL* parodied The Troggs tapes with a medieval musical sketch featuring Shaffer, Bill Murray, Harry Shearer, and a "special guest appearance" by John Belushi. In the middle of a long tirade using numerous repetitions of the word "flogging", Shaffer inadvertently uttered "fucking" instead. This was not removed by the censors in the live broadcast and the West Coast taped airing, and reappeared in the summer rerun and the syndicated versions of the show for several years.

Films

Films based on *SNL* sketches are listed below with their release, budget, gross, and ratings from Rotten Tomatoes and Metacritic. The gross is from Box Office Mojo. A Rotten Tomatoes score of 60% or higher indicates the film is "fresh" (well-received); Metacritic scores from 81–100, 61–80, 40–60, 20–39, and 0–19 indicate near-universal acclaim, generally favorable reviews, mixed reviews, poor reviews, and overwhelming dislike, respectively. IMDb ratings are from 1 to 10, 10 being the best; these ratings are subject to change over time.

Film	Release date	Budget	Worldwide gross	Rotten Tomatoes rating	Metacritic rating	IMDb rating	MPAA rating	Distributor
The Blues Brothers	June 20, 1980	$27 million	$115,229,890	84% (fresh)	-	7.9	R	Universal
Wayne's World	February 14, 1992	$20 million	$183,097,323	83% (fresh)	53	6.9	PG-13	Paramount
Wayne's World 2	December 10, 1993	$40 million	$48,197,805	59%	-	5.8	PG-13	Paramount
Coneheads	July 23, 1993	TBA	$21,274,717	27%	-	5.0	PG	Paramount
It's Pat	August 26, 1994	TBA	$60,822	0%	-	2.4	PG-13	Buena Vista
Stuart Saves His Family	April 14, 1995	$15 million	$912,082	29%	-	5.0	PG-13	Paramount
A Night at the Roxbury	October 2, 1998	$17 million	$30,331,165	10%	26	5.7	PG-13	Paramount
Blues Brothers 2000	February 6, 1998	$28 million	$14,051,384	45%	-	4.4	PG-13	Universal
Superstar	October 8, 1999	$14 million	$30,636,478	33%	42	4.5	PG-13	Paramount
The Ladies Man	October 13, 2000	$24 million	$13,616,610	11%	22	4.7	R	Paramount
MacGruber	May 21, 2010	$10 million	$9,259,314	47%	43	7.0	R	Universal

The early days of *SNL* spawned several films, including the successful *The Blues Brothers* (1980). However, it was the success of *Wayne's World* (1992) that encouraged Lorne Michaels to produce more film spin-offs, based on several popular sketch characters. Michaels revived 1970s characters for *Coneheads* (1993), followed by *It's Pat* (1994); *Stuart Saves His Family* (1995, with the Stuart Smalley character); *A Night at the Roxbury* (1998, with the Butabi Brothers characters); *Superstar* (1999, with the Mary Katherine Gallagher character); and *The Ladies Man* (2000). Some did moderately well, though others did not—notably, *It's Pat*, which did so badly at the box office that the studio which made the film, Touchstone Pictures (owned by The Walt Disney Company, which also owns NBC's rival ABC), pulled it only one week after releasing it, and *Stuart Saves His Family*, with the latter losing US$15 million. Many of these films were produced by Paramount Pictures. The films based on *The Blues Brothers* were produced by Universal Studios, which merged with NBC in 2004 to form NBC Universal (Universal also has a joint venture with Paramount for international distribution of the two studios' films).

In addition, *Office Space* (1999) originated from a series of Mike Judge animated short films that aired on *SNL* after appearing on several other programs.

The character Bob Roberts from the Tim Robbins film of the same name, first appeared on *SNL* in a short film about the conservative folk singer.

The group The Folksmen first appeared on *SNL*, performing the song "Old Joe's Place" before later appearing in the film *A Mighty Wind*. The three members of the Folksmen were the same three comedians: Harry Shearer, Michael McKean, and Christopher Guest, who also appeared on the same episode as the rock group Spinal Tap. At the time of the appearance (the 1984–85 season), Shearer and Guest were cast members.

Awards

Main article: List of awards and nominations received by Saturday Night Live

Saturday Night Live has won numerous awards since its debut, including 21 Primetime Emmy Awards, 1 Peabody Award, and 3 Writers Guild of America Awards. In 2002, it was ranked tenth on TV Guide's 50 Greatest TV Shows of All Time, while in 2007 it was honored with inclusion on *Time* magazine's list of "100 Best TV Shows of All-*TIME*."

Merchandise

DVD

Main article: List of Saturday Night Live DVD releases

Currently, Universal Studios Home Entertainment and Lions Gate Entertainment hold video rights to the series. Universal has issued complete season DVD sets to the first few seasons, while Lionsgate's share of the rights are a result of prior contracts with NBC struck before the NBC Universal merger. A majority of Lionsgate's SNL DVDs are "Best Of..." compilations.

Books

The first authorized book for the series was published by Avon Books in 1977. *Saturday Night Live* (ISBN 0380018012) was edited by Anne Beatts and John Head, with photography by Edie Baskin; all three worked for *Saturday Night Live* at the time the book was published. The oversized illustrated paperback included the scripts for several sketches by the Not Ready for Prime Time Players, as the repertory cast was known at first.

Criticism and controversy

Censorship

In some cases, a sketch was censored in repeat broadcasts.

- In a November 21, 1992, "Wayne's World" sketch, the characters Wayne and Garth (respectively portrayed by Mike Myers and Dana Carvey) made fun of Chelsea Clinton (the then 12-year-old daughter of the then President-elect Bill Clinton), implying that Chelsea was incapable of causing males to "Schwing!". This joke was subsequently edited out of all repeats and syndication rebroadcasts of this sketch.
- The 1998 Robert Smigel animated short film "Conspiracy Theory Rock", part of a March 1998 "TV Funhouse" segment, has been removed from all subsequent airings of the SNL episode where it originally appeared. Michaels claimed the edit was done because it "wasn't funny". The film is a scathing critique of corporate media ownership, including NBC's ownership by General Electric/Westinghouse.

Ashlee Simpson incident

Simpson appeared as a musical guest on October 23, 2004, and, as is customary for the show's format, she was scheduled to perform two songs. Her first song, "Pieces of Me," was performed without problems. However, when she began her second song, "Autobiography," the vocals for the song "Pieces of Me" were heard again—before she had even raised the microphone to her mouth. Simpson began to do an impromptu jig when she realized the embarrassing error, but then left the stage. During the closing of the show Simpson appeared with the guest host Jude Law and said, "I'm so sorry. My band started playing the wrong song, and I didn't know what to do, so I thought I'd do a hoedown."

On October 25, Simpson called in to the music video show *Total Request Live* and explained that due to complications arising from severe acid reflux disease, which had previously been seen bothering her in *The Ashlee Simpson Show*, she had completely lost her voice and her doctor had advised her not to sing. She said that because of the acid reflux, her father wanted her to use a vocal guide track for the performance. Simpson stated of the incident, "I made a complete fool of myself." According to Simpson, the drummer hit the wrong button, which caused the wrong track to be played. During the October 25 Radio Music Awards broadcast, Simpson pretended, as a joke, to make the same mistake as she did in the *SNL* incident, but then began to perform "Autobiography" without using a pre-recorded vocal track as she had done during the prior *SNL* performance. On October 31, the CBS news program *60 Minutes* aired footage from Simpson's rehearsals before the *SNL* performance in which Simpson is shown to be disturbed by poor voice control.

When Jude Law hosted for the second time in season 35 on March 13, 2010, with musical guest Pearl Jam, he referenced the incident, saying "You know, last time I was here, my musical guest was Ashlee Simpson. And you know what? I think she was great!" Law mouthed the "I think she was great!" part, while a pre-recorded voice of his played over the loudspeakers.

Sinéad O'Connor incident

On October 3, 1992, Sinéad O'Connor appeared on *SNL* as the musical guest. She was singing an a cappella version of Bob Marley's "War," which she intended as a protest over the sexual abuse in the Roman Catholic Church, by changing the lyric "racism" to "child abuse." She then presented a photo of Pope John Paul II to the camera while singing the word "evil", after which she tore the photo into pieces, said "Fight the real enemy," and threw the pieces towards the camera.

Saturday Night Live had no foreknowledge of O'Connor's plan. As of 2010, NBC still declines to rebroadcast the sequence with the exception of an interview with O'Connor on MSNBC's The Rachel Maddow Show which aired on 24 April 2010 when MSNBC aired the full clip during the interview. NBC replaced the incident with footage from the dress rehearsal where O'Connor holds a photo of an African child before bowing and leaving the stage. The dress rehearsal version is also used for 60-minute syndicated rebroadcasts (seen on Comedy Central and E! Entertainment Television). However, the original episode is available on volume four of the *SNL* DVD special *"Saturday Night Live - 25 Years of Music"*, with an introduction by show creator/executive producer Lorne Michaels about the incident.

Rage Against the Machine incident

On April 13, 1996, the band Rage Against the Machine were the musical guests, and were scheduled to perform two songs. The show was hosted that night by ex-Republican presidential candidate and billionaire Steve Forbes. According to RATM guitarist Tom Morello, "RATM wanted to stand in sharp juxtaposition to a billionaire telling jokes and promoting his flat tax by making our own statement." To this end, the band hung two upside-down American flags from their amplifiers. Seconds before they took the stage to perform "Bulls on Parade", *SNL* and NBC sent stagehands in to pull the flags down. Following the removal of the flags during the first performance, the band was approached by *SNL* and NBC officials and ordered to immediately leave the building. Upon hearing this, bassist Tim Commerford reportedly stormed Forbes' dressing room, throwing shreds from one of the torn down flags. Morello noted that members of the *Saturday Night Live* cast and crew, whom he declined to name, "[e]xpressed solidarity with our actions, and a sense of shame that their show had censored the performance."

Further reading

- Cader, Michael. (1994). *Saturday Night Live: The First Twenty Years*. Boston, MA: Houghton Mifflin. ISBN 0-395-70895-8.
- Hill, Doug, and Jeff Weingrad. (1986). *Saturday Night: A Backstage History of Saturday Night Live*. New York, NY: Beech Tree Books. ISBN 0-688-05099-9.
- Mohr, Jay. (2004). *Gasping for Airtime: Two Years in the Trenches of Saturday Night Live*. New York, NY: Hyperion. ISBN 1-4013-0006-5.
- Shales, Tom, and James Andrew Miller. (2002). *Live from New York: An Uncensored History of Saturday Night Live*. Boston, MA: Little, Brown. ISBN 0-316-78146-0.
- Streeter, Michael. (2005). *Nothing Lost Forever: The Films of Tom Schiller*. New York, NY: BearManor Media. ISBN 1593930321.

External links

- Official NBC website [1]
- Official website [2] for Broadway Video
- Saturday Night Live: Early Years [3] - slideshow by *Life (magazine)*
- *Saturday Night Live* [4] at the Internet Movie Database
- *Saturday Night Live* [5] at TV.com
- *SNL* Transcripts [6] from snltranscripts.jt.org
- Saturday Night Live Cast and Musical guest database [7] from snlmusic.parshaparts.com

Lorne's Production Company

Broadway Video

Type	Private
Industry	Entertainment
Founded	1979
Headquarters	New York, USA
Key people	Lorne Michaels, Jack Sullivan (CEO), Joseph Brady (CFO), Ralph Kelsey (Vice-President, Broadway Sound), Cristina McGinniss (President, Broadway Video Editorial), Kathryn Miller (Senior Vice President), Britta von Schoeler (Senior Vice President and General Manager, Broadway Video Enterprises), Michael Ungar (Vice President, Broadway Sound)
Products	Motion pictures, television programs
Revenue	$27.3M (US)
Employees	130
Website	broadwayvideo.com [1]

Broadway Video is a media production and distribution company located within the Brill Building on Broadway, New York, United States. Founded in 1979 as a production house tasked with post-production work on *Saturday Night Live,* Broadway Video has since become one of the largest independent production companies within New York. It has won several awards, including an Emmy for production work on the television program *30 Rock.*

The company was founded by Lorne Michaels in 1979. In addition to an increased focus on distribution, Broadway Video increased its production of television series, typically starring *Saturday Night Live* alums. The company saw its first major success with the release of the primetime NBC comedy series, *30 Rock.*

Broadway Video is an independent entertainment company. With headquarters in New York, and offices in Los Angeles, are responsible for the production and distribution of numerous television and film titles. Founded by Lorne Michaels in 1979, the initial focus of the company was the handling of post-production duties of NBC's *Saturday Night Live*. Subsequently, Broadway Video has expanded into the production and select distribution of television and film titles in a variety of genres. More recently, Broadway Video has been involved in the production of short-form media, including television commercials and broadcast promotions.

In 2009, Broadway Video Entertainment was issued the trademark rights to "Broadway Video" by the USPTO.

Divisions

Broadway Video Editorial

In 2009 Broadway Video bolstered their production division through the heavy expansion of services through the increased hiring of personnel, with the aim of consolidating all production duties "in-house". September 2009 saw Broadway Video hiring noted editors Rick Barlis, Anthony Gianni, and Dan Fisher. These hirings strengthened the company's relationship with NBC, in particular, its sibling channel, Syfy. Broadway Video was responsible for the large-scale rebranding of the channel from the previously known Sci Fi to Syfy through the Imagine Greater campaign.

The design division is currently headed by Creative Director Katherine Burke, with the group having worked with numerous corporate clients, including NBC, Showtime, and USA Networks. Currently held advertising accounts include American Express and Procter & Gamble.

In addition to those individuals already mentioned, notable editing personnel include Scott Cumbo, Dave Finamore, Yossi Kimberg, and Christine McLean.

Following previous informal collaborations, in 2009 it was announced that Frantic Studios would consolidate their operations into Broadway Video's New York offices. Frantic Studios, with Creative Director David Sutton, specialize in broadcast and advertising productions. In July 2009, Frantic Studios won a CINE Golden Eagle Award for their work for CBS News.

Broadway Sound

Working closely with Broadway Production Services, Broadway Sound provides full post-production facilities, with the division founded in 1995 by Mike Ungar and Ralph Kelsey. Studios are ADR (Automated Dialogue Replacement) capable, with original music compositions, performance, production and audio restoration handled in partnership with SandBlast Productions. Current Head of Operations is Monnel Cremin, with Kim Feit acting as Business Manager. Notable production staff include Kevin McElligott, Mike Garatty, Andrew Avitabile, Sean Canada, Shane Conry, John Crenshaw, and Vince Verderame.

Broadway Video Enterprises

Broadway Video Enterprises manages the distribution of Broadway Video Entertainment's existing program library across all media channels. The library contains over 1,000 hours of programming including "The Kids in the Hall," "Saturday Night Live," and more. Enterprises' distribution efforts have resulted in a huge international presence for "SNL." The series airs in approximately 130 countries worldwide, including Italy and Spain where the licensed format is the basis of successful local series. SNL's consumer products line tops 240 items including nearly 30 DVD titles. SNL has significantly impacted the digital space and receives millions of video views each week on Hulu and NBC.com. The SNL Digital Short "Lazy Sunday" led to YouTube's 83% jump in market share of video search users back in 2006. Another SNL Digital Short, "Dick in a Box," has been streamed over 40M times, and SNL's election coverage was credited for driving the immense growth of online video in the fourth quarter of 2008.

Broadway Video Television

Responsible for the production of prime-time television series, Broadway Video Television was established in 2003 in Los Angeles. Prior to this, television productions were handled in tandem by numerous divisions of Broadway Video. The initial, and on-going, production for the division was the critically-acclaimed 30 Rock, with Late Night with Jimmy Fallon following in 2009. Additionally in 2009, concurrent with the beginning of the 35th season, Broadway Video Television absorbed partial production duties of *Saturday Night Live*.

Selected productions

Below is a select list of audio, film, and television projects in which Broadway Video has been involved. Only those projects where the company has had a major role, such as in the production or distribution process, have been included.

Audio

Title	Artist	Release Date	Status	Role	Notes
Incredibad	The Lonely Island	2009	Released	Distribution	
Ridiculous	Norm McDonald	2006	Released	Distribution	
They're All Gonna Laugh at You!	Adam Sandler	1993	Released	Distribution	
What's Your Name?	Adam Sandler	1997	Released	Distribution	
What the Hell Happened to Me?	Adam Sandler	1996	Released	Distribution	

Film

Title	Release Date	Status	Role	Notes
80 Blocks from Tiffany's	1979	Released	Distribution	
Baby Mama	2008	Released	Production	
Black Sheep	1996	Released	Production	
Enigma	2001	Released	Production	
The Gatling Gun	1973	Released	Production	
Hot Rod	2007	Released	Production	
Key Party	2010 (Tentative)	In Development	Production	
Lassie	1994	Released	Production	
MacGruber	2010	Released	Production	
Mean Girls	2004	Released	Production	
The Rutles: All You Need Is Cash	1978	Released	Production, Distribution	
The Rutles 2: You Can't Buy Me Lunch	2002	Released	Production	

Television

Title	Release Date	Status	Role	Notes
30 Rock	2006	Released	Production	
The Beach Boys Good Vibration Tour	2005	Released	Distribution	
The Best of the Blues Brothers	1993	Released	Distribution	
Bob & Ray, Jane, Laraine & Gilda	1981	Released	Distribution	
Candles, Snow & Mistletoe	1993	Released	Distribution	
The Coneheads	1983	Released	Production	
Countdown to the Emmys	2002	Released	Production	
Diary of a Young Comic	1979	Released	Distribution	
Doll Day Afternoon	1987	Released	Production	
Franken & Davis at Stockton State	1984	Released	Distribution	
A Freezerburnt Christmas	1997	Released	Production	

Title	Year	Status	Role	Notes
Frosty Returns	1992	Released	Production	
Kids in the Hall	1988	Released	Production, Distribution	
Kids in the Hall: Brain Candy	1996	Released	Production	
Neil Young in Berlin	1986	Released	Distribution	
Late Night with Conan O'Brien	2003	Released	Production	
Late Night with Jimmy Fallon	2009	Released	Production	
The Line	2008	Released	Production, Distribution	
Lookwell	1991	Abandoned	Production	Did not proceed to series
Macy's 4th of July Fireworks Spectacular	2000	Released	Production	
Mr. Mike's Mondo Video	1979	Released	Distribution	Was pulled before airing in 1979
Mr. Miller Goes to Washington Starring Dennis Miller	1988	Released	Production	
Name That Video	2001	Released	Production	
The New Show	1984	Released	Distribution	
Night Music	1977	Released	Distribution	
Night of Too Many Stars	2003	Released	Production	
The Paul Simon Special	1977	Released	Distribution	
Randy Newman - Live at the Odeon	1983	Released	Distribution	
Second Star to the Left	2001	Released	Production	
Sons & Daughters	2006	Released	Production	
SportsCentury: The Century's Greatest Athletes	2002	Released	Production	
Steve Martin's Best Show Ever	1981	Released	Production	
Strange Frequency	2001	Released	Production	
Strange Frequency 2	2001	Released	Production	
Sunday Night/Night Music	1988	Released	Production, Distribution	
Things We Did Last Summer	1978	Released	Production, Distribution	
Toonces, The Cat Who Could Drive a Car	1992	Released	Production	

The Tracey Morgan Show	2003	Released	Production	
The Vacant Lot	1993	Released	Distribution	
Wulin Warriors: Legend of the Seven Stars/Thunder Force	2006	Released	Distribution	Acquired worldwide television, merchandising, and homevideo rights

Location

The headquarters of Broadway Video are located within the Brill Building on 1619 Broadway, New York. All divisions of the company are housed in this location, with the exception of Broadway Video Television, which is located in Los Angeles.

1619 Broadway, New York, also known as the Brill Building, is the headquarters of Broadway Video.

See also

- Lorne Michaels
- NBC
- *Saturday Night Live*
- SNL Studios

External links

- Broadway Video Official Site [1]
- Broadway Video [2] at the Internet Movie Database
- Broadway Pictures [3] at the Internet Movie Database

Great Comedies Produced by Lorne

Three Amigos

¡Three Amigos!	
Theatrical release poster	
Directed by	John Landis
Produced by	Lorne Michaels George Folsey, Jr.
Written by	Lorne Michaels Steve Martin Randy Newman
Starring	Chevy Chase Steve Martin Martin Short
Music by	Elmer Bernstein (score) Randy Newman (songs)
Cinematography	Ronald W. Browne
Editing by	Malcolm Campbell
Studio	HBO Films
Distributed by	Orion Pictures
Release date(s)	December 12, 1986
Running time	104 minutes
Country	United States
Language	English
Budget	$25 million
Gross revenue	$39,246,734

Three Amigos (marketed as ***¡Three Amigos!***) is a 1986 American adventure musical comedy film directed by John Landis and written by Lorne Michaels, Steve Martin, and Randy Newman. Chevy Chase, Steve Martin, and Martin Short star as the title characters, three silent film stars who are mistaken for real heroes by a small Mexican village and must find a way to live up to that reputation.

The film is number 79 on Bravo's "100 Funniest Movies."

Plot

The film opens as a bandit named El Guapo (Alfonso Arau) and his gang of thugs have been collecting protection money from the small Mexican village of Santo Poco. Carmen (Patrice Martinez), daughter of the village leader, searches for someone who can come to the rescue of her townspeople. While visiting a small village church, she remains to watch a silent film featuring "The Three Amigos" and, believing them to be real heroes, sends a telegram to Hollywood asking them to come and stop El Guapo. However, the telegraph operator edits her message down since she has very little money to pay for it.

Meanwhile, Lucky Day (Steve Martin), Dusty Bottoms (Chevy Chase), and Ned Nederlander (Martin Short) are Hollywood silent film actors who portray the heroic Three Amigos on screen in 1916. When they demand a salary increase, studio boss Harry Flugleman (Joe Mantegna) fires them and evicts them from their studio-owned housing. Shortly afterward, they receive Carmen's telegram, but misinterpret it as an invitation to make a film with El Guapo. After breaking into the studio to retrieve their costumes, the Amigos head for Mexico. Stopping at a cantina near Santo Poco, they are mistaken for associates of a fast-shooting German pilot (Kai Wulff), who is also looking for El Guapo and who arrived just before they did. A relieved Carmen picks up the Amigos and takes them to the village, where they are put up in the best house in town and treated very well. The next morning, when three of El Guapo's men come to raid the village, the Amigos do a Hollywood-style stunt show that leaves them very confused. The bandits ride off, making everyone think that the Amigos have defeated the enemy; in reality, the men inform El Guapo of what has happened, and he decides to return in force the next day and kill the Amigos.

As the German's real associates arrive at the cantina, proving themselves just as adept with pistols as he is, the village throws a boisterous celebration for the Amigos and their (supposed) victory. The next morning, El Guapo and his gang come to Santo Poco and call out the Amigos, who confess that they have only been acting and are too scared to confront him after Lucky gets shot in the arm. El Guapo allows his men to loot the village and kidnaps Carmen, and the Amigos leave Santo Poco in disgrace. With nothing waiting for them back home, Ned persuades Lucky and Dusty to become real-life heroes and go after El Guapo. Their first attempt to find his hideout fails, but they spot a cargo plane and follow it to him; the plane is flown by the German, who has brought a shipment of rifles for the gang with his associates' help. Preparations are underway for El Guapo's 40th birthday party, and he plans to make Carmen his bride. The Amigos try to sneak into the hideout, with mixed results: Lucky is captured and chained up in a dungeon, Dusty crashes through a window and into Carmen's room, and Ned ends up hanging among the decorations.

As Lucky frees himself and Dusty sneaks out only to be caught, Ned falls loose and is also captured. The German, having idolized Ned's quick-draw pistol skills since childhood, challenges him to a showdown. Ned wins, killing the German, and Lucky holds El Guapo at gunpoint long enough for Carmen and the Amigos to escape — first on horseback, then in the German's plane. Returning to Santo Poco with El Guapo's entire army in pursuit, they rally the villagers to stand up for themselves and plan a defense. The bandits arrive in the seemingly empty village, only to find themselves suddenly being shot at by Amigos from all sides and falling into hidden water-filled trenches dug by the villagers. Eventually all of El Guapo's men either desert him or die in the gunfire, and he takes a fatal wound as well. As he lies dying, the villagers — all armed and wearing replicas of the Amigos' costumes — step out to confront him. El Guapo congratulates them on this plan, then shoots Lucky in the foot and dies.

The villagers offer to give the Amigos all the money they have, but the Amigos refuse it, saying (as in their movies) that seeing justice done is enough of a reward for them. They then ride off into the sunset, ready to continue being real heroes.

Cast

- Chevy Chase as Dusty Bottoms
- Steve Martin as Lucky Day
- Martin Short as Ned Nederlander
- Alfonso Arau as El Guapo
- Tony Plana as Jefe
- Joe Mantegna as Harry Flugleman
- Kai Wulff as the German
- Patrice Martinez as Carmen
- Norbert Weisser and Brian Thompson as the German's friends
- Randy Newman as the Singing Bush
- Phil Hartman and Jon Lovitz make cameo appearances as Sam and Morty, Harry Flugleman's assistants

Production

The film was written by Martin, Michaels, and Randy Newman. Newman contributed three original songs: "The Ballad of the Three Amigos", "My Little Buttercup", and "Blue Shadows," while the musical score was composed by Elmer Bernstein. It was shot in Simi Valley, California, Coronado National Forest, Old Tucson Studios, and Hollywood.[citation needed]

Reception

The movie received mixed reviews. Noted film critic Roger Ebert said "The ideas to make *Three Amigos* into a good comedy are here, but the madness is missing." It holds a 56% "rotten" rating on review aggregator Rotten Tomatoes. It has a rating of 6.0/10 on IMDB. It was ranked #79 on Bravo's list of the "100 Funniest Movies".

External links

- *¡Three Amigos!* [1] at the Internet Movie Database
- *¡Three Amigos!* [2] at Box Office Mojo
- *¡Three Amigos!* [3] at Rotten Tomatoes

Coneheads (film)

Coneheads	
Coneheads poster	
Directed by	Steve Barron
Produced by	Lorne Michaels
Written by	Tom Davis Dan Aykroyd Bonnie Turner Terry Turner
Starring	Dan Aykroyd Jane Curtin David Spade Michael McKean
Music by	David Newman
Cinematography	Francis Kenny [1]
Editing by	Paul Trejo
Distributed by	Paramount Pictures
Release date(s)	July 23, 1993
Running time	88 min.
Country	United States
Language	English

Gross revenue	Domestic: $21,274,717

Coneheads is the title of a 1993 film based on the *Saturday Night Live* sketches about the Coneheads. The film was directed by Steve Barron and produced by Lorne Michaels. As was the case with the previous SNL skit-inspired film *The Blues Brothers*, *Coneheads* has been said to have made an "accidental" or "unintentional" political statement or social commentary about the nature of the immigrant experience in America, the filmmakers' ostensible intent being merely to entertain.[citation needed] **Coneheads** remains the only SNL film in history to receive a PG rating.

The film stars Dan Aykroyd and Jane Curtin as Beldar and Prymaat Clorhone (who later Anglicize their Remulakian surname to "Conehead"), parents of Connie (Michelle Burke, taking over the role played by Laraine Newman on *SNL*). Michael McKean and David Spade play INS officials; also appearing are Sinbad and *SNL* alumni Phil Hartman, Jan Hooks, Tim Meadows, Jon Lovitz, Peter Aykroyd, Tom Davis, Garrett Morris, Chris Farley, Laraine Newman, Kevin Nealon, Julia Sweeney, and Adam Sandler.

Other supporting cast members include Jason Alexander and Lisa Jane Persky. Alexander's *Seinfeld* co-star, Michael Richards, makes a cameo appearance, as do Eddie Griffin, Joey Lauren Adams, Parker Posey, Ellen DeGeneres, Drew Carey, Dave Thomas, and Tom Arnold.

The movie largely took place in Paramus, New Jersey, with scenes also shot in New York City and the New Jersey towns of Jersey City, and Wrightstown.

Plot

The film follows the adventures of the family - whose ship, as part of an advance scouting mission for an invasion, is shot down by an F-16 fighter-interceptor of the New Jersey Air National Guard, and they try to assimilate into American society and pursue the immigrant's American dream. They live with secret identities while an INS agent tracks them incessantly over the years. They blend into a community and take up activities that are part and parcel of the American Dream. They also deal with their teenage daughter dating. At the end Beldar is allowed by an INS agent to remain on Earth provided Beldar can demonstrate a skill that no one else can.

Cast

- Dan Aykroyd as Beldar Conehead / Donald R. DeCicco
- Jane Curtin as Prymaat Conehead / Mary Margaret Rowney
- Michael Richards as Motel Clerk
- Eddie Griffin as Customer
- Sinbad as Otto
- Phil Hartman as Marlax
- Adam Sandler as Carmine Weiner
- David Spade as Eli Turnbull, INS Agent
- Michael McKean as Gorman Seedling, INS Agent
- Mitchell Bobrow as Garthok Combatant
- Chris Farley as Ronnie Bradford the Mechanic
- Jason Alexander as Larry Farber
- Lisa Jane Persky as Lisa Farber
- Michelle Burke as Connie Conehead
- Drew Carey as Taxi Passenger
- Kevin Nealon as Senator
- Parker Posey as Stephanie
- Joey Lauren Adams as Christina
- Julia Sweeney as Principal
- Ellen DeGeneres as Coach
- Tim Meadows as Athletic Cone
- Jonathan Penner as Captain Air Traffic
- Whip Hubley as F-16 Pilot
- Jon Lovitz as Dr. Rudolph, dentist (uncredited)
- Tom Arnold as Golfer (uncredited) (Tom Arnold's character is the only person, in either the film or any of the sketches, to actually question the shape of Beldar's head, while everyone else remains strangely oblivious.)

Soundtrack

Coneheads: Music From The Motion Picture Soundtrack	
Soundtrack by Various Artists	
Released	July 20, 1993
Genre	Soundtrack
Length	43:27
Label	Warner Bros. Records

The soundtrack for *Coneheads* was released July 20, 1993.

1. "Magic Carpet Ride" by Michael Monroe & Slash
2. "Tainted Love" by Soft Cell
3. "No More Tears (Enough Is Enough)" by Andy Bell & k.d. lang
4. "Kodachrome" by Paul Simon
5. "Can't Take My Eyes off You" by Morten Harket
6. "It's a Free World, Baby" by R.E.M.
7. "Soul to Squeeze" by Red Hot Chili Peppers
8. "Fight the Power" by Barenaked Ladies
9. "Little Renee" by Digable Planets
10. "Chale Jao" by Babble
11. "Conehead Love" by Nan Schaefer

External links

- *Coneheads* [2] at the Internet Movie Database

Wayne's World (film)

Wayne's World	
Theatrical release poster	
Directed by	Penelope Spheeris
Produced by	Hawk Koch Lorne Michaels
Written by	Mike Myers Bonnie Turner Terry Turner
Starring	Mike Myers Dana Carvey Rob Lowe Tia Carrere
Music by	J. Peter Robinson
Cinematography	Theo van de Sande
Editing by	Malcolm Campbell
Distributed by	Paramount Pictures
Release date(s)	February 14, 1992
Running time	95 minutes
Country	United States
Language	English
Budget	$20,000,000
Gross revenue	$121,697,323 (domestically), $183,097,323 (worldwide)
Followed by	*Wayne's World 2*

Wayne's World is a 1992 comedy film starring Mike Myers as Wayne Campbell and Dana Carvey as Garth Algar, hosts of the Aurora, Illinois-based cable access television show *Wayne's World*. The film was adapted from a sketch of the same name on NBC's *Saturday Night Live*.

The film grossed US$121.6 million in its theatrical run, placing it as the tenth highest-grossing film of 1992 and the highest-grossing film ever based on a *Saturday Night Live* skit. It was directed by Penelope Spheeris, with Myers co-writing the script.

Wayne's World was Myers' feature film debut. The film also featured Rob Lowe, Tia Carrere, Lara Flynn Boyle, Brian Doyle-Murray, Robert Patrick (spoofing his role in *Terminator 2: Judgment Day*),

Ed O'Neill, Ione Skye, Meat Loaf, and Alice Cooper.

Wayne's World received mostly positive reviews upon release and was commercially successful (unlike many *Saturday Night Live*-based films). Filmed in just 34 days, it was followed by *Wayne's World 2*. In 2003, readers of *Total Film* magazine voted *Wayne's World* the 41st greatest comedy film of all time.

Summary

Wayne Campbell (Myers) and Garth Algar (Carvey) are the hosts of Wayne's World, a local Friday late-night cable access program based in Aurora, Illinois, where they ogle pictures of beautiful celebrity women, play air guitar and drums, and interview local people, indirectly making fun of them over the course of the interview. The program is popular with local viewers. One day Benjamin Kane (Lowe), a television station executive, is visiting a girlfriend (Ione Skye) who turns the TV to the show. When she tells him how many people watch the show, he instructs his producer Russell Finley (Kurt Fuller) to find out where the show is taped, telling him they may have an opportunity for a huge sponsorship.

Benjamin shows up next week in Wayne's basement and introduces himself after the show ends. He offers to buy the rights to the show for $10,000 ($5,000 each) and to keep Wayne and Garth on for what he describes as a "huge" salary. Garth then covertly speaks to the audience, sensing he has a bad feeling that Wayne is selling out, but he is too shy to confront Wayne about it. Following the purchase of the show, it is quickly "reinvented", complete with a weekly interview guaranteed to Noah Vanderhoff (Brian Doyle-Murray), the show's sponsor. The first reinvented show is also their last, as Wayne holds up a series of cards with questions on the front and, unknowingly to Vanderhoff, insulting phrases on the back such as "Sphincter Boy" (with an arrow pointing at Vanderhoff), "He blows goats...I have proof" and "This man has no penis", prompting Benjamin to call Wayne up to the control booth and fire him on the spot.

At the same time, Wayne's blossoming relationship with hard rock vocalist and bassist Cassandra (Tia Carrere), the frontwoman of a band named Crucial Taunt, leads to a rift forming between Wayne and Garth. It erupts after Wayne walks out on the show, leaving Garth to a bout of stage fright for the rest of the show. The two separate, but later make up after Wayne breaks up with Cassandra following an argument between them over Benjamin.

While making up with Garth, Wayne remembers a limo belonging to record executive Frankie Sharp (Frank DiLeo) outside a concert of Alice Cooper in Milwaukee. He also remembers that a security guard at the concert (Chris Farley) said that Sharp would be riding through Chicago later that day and forms a plan with Garth to get her back. With everyone in the donut shop helping, Wayne is able to convince Cassandra, who is at a video shoot directed by Benjamin, to leave the shoot with the band and head back to Aurora with him to perform on the show. Garth, meanwhile, hacks into a satellite system and is able to route the signal from the broadcast into the television set in Sharp's limo. In the meantime, the police keep Benjamin at bay and leave him unable to enter the house until the show's over.

Nearing the end of Cassandra's song, Frankie Sharp and Benjamin enter the basement. Once the song is finished, these endings occur:

- Frankie says to Cassandra that it is the wrong time to sign her band, causing her to become infuriated with Wayne. Wayne is called small-time by Benjamin just before he leaves with Cassandra, and Stacy comes in to announce to Wayne that she is pregnant. Suddenly, an electrical fire starts from the broadcasting equipment and consumes the house. While Wayne walks out of the burned-down house with a dead Garth, Cassandra lies in paradise with Benjamin while he remarks "You didn't really think she'd end up with Wayne, did you?" (The Sad ending)
- Wayne pulls off Benjamin's face, revealing that he's actually Old Man Withers, who then remarks, true to Scooby-Doo form, "And I would have gotten away with it, too, if it hadn't been for you meddling kids!" (The Scooby-Doo ending)
- Frankie gives Cassandra a six album record deal, Wayne and Cassandra kiss, Russell and one of the crew members who keeps saying "I love you" get together, while he announces how he discovered that "platonic love can exist between two grown men", Noah mentions that he's glad people are seeing him in a new light, Benjamin realizes being successful doesn't get you everything, and Garth finally gets with his dream girl. (The Mega-Happy ending) [Note: This ending is canonical in relation to the continuity of the second film]

Cast

- **Mike Myers** as Wayne Campbell
- **Dana Carvey** as Garth Algar
- **Tia Carrere** as Cassandra Wong
- **Rob Lowe** as Benjamin Kane
- **Lara Flynn Boyle** as Stacy, Wayne's ex-girlfriend
- **Michael DeLuise** as Alan, one of Wayne and Garth's crew
- **Lee Tergesen** as Terry, Wayne and Garth's cameraman
- **Sean Gregory Sullivan** as Phil, Wayne and Garth's friend who works at a garage
- **Brian Doyle-Murray** as video arcade magnate Noah Vanderhoff
- **Colleen Camp** as his wife, Mrs. Vanderhoff
- **Kurt Fuller** as Russell Finley, Benjamin's assistant
- **Chris Farley** as the well-informed security guard at the back of Alice Cooper concert
- **Frank DiLeo** as rock promoter Frankie 'Mr. Big' Sharp
- **Ed O'Neill** as Glen, the manager at Stan Mikita's Donuts
- **Mike Hagerty** as Davy, a controller at the Cable 10 television station who Benjamin and Russell ask for help, he later claims that he got laid off while at Stan Mikita's.
- **Frederick Coffin** as Officer Koharski
- **Donna Dixon** as Garth's dream woman

- **Ione Skye** as Elyse, Benjamin's girlfriend, who introduces him to Wayne's World
- **Robin Ruzan** as a waitress.
- **Charles Noland** as Ron Paxton, who tries to market his invention, the "Suck-Kut", to Garth
- **Carmen Filpi** as Old Man Withers
- **Chaz Healy** as Concert-goer
- **Alice Cooper** as himself
- **Pete Friesen** as himself, Alice Cooper's guitarist
- **Derek Sherinian** as himself, Alice Cooper's keyboard player
- **Jimmy DeGrasso** as himself, Alice Cooper's drummer
- **Robert Patrick** reprising his role in Terminator 2.

Effect on pop culture

Filled with pop culture references, the sketches and film started catchphrases such as "*Schwing!*" and "Schyea", as well as popularizing "That's what she said", "Party on!" and the use of "...Not!" after apparently affirmative sentences in order to state the contrary (as used by the metal band Anthrax in the late 1980s and early 1990s). It augmented the slacker language of Generation X, much as *Bill & Ted's Excellent Adventure* had done previously. It featured a baby blue 1976 AMC Pacer with flames and non-matching wheels, which Wayne and Garth dubbed "The Mirthmobile".

The film frequently breaks the fourth wall, with Wayne, Garth, and others on occasion speaking directly to the audience. Parts of the story are carried by Wayne's narration to the camera, in which he offers his thoughts on what's happening in the film. Despite Wayne, Garth, Cassandra, Glen, and Ben addressing the viewer, no one else seems aware that they are in a film.

Wayne's World AMC Pacer clone at Planet Hollywood in New York City

Video games

In 1993, a *Wayne's World* video game was released for the Nintendo Entertainment System, Super Nintendo Entertainment System, the Sega Mega Drive, and the Nintendo Game Boy. The game's plot differs from the film: the player controls Wayne as he goes on a mission throughout Aurora – visiting The Gas Works, Stan Mikita's, and the music store from the "No Stairway" scene, among other locations – to rescue Garth from inside the "Zoltar the Gelatinous Cube" arcade game mentioned in the film.

Alternatively, an adventure game version of Wayne's World was released around the same time for DOS. The plot involves Wayne and Garth trying to raise money to save their show by holding a "pizza-thon".

In the beginning of the film, the Noah's Arcade commercial features Starlight Zone from Sonic the Hedgehog playing behind Noah Vanderhoff, the owner of the Noah's Arcade franchise.

In addition, Grand Theft Auto IV: The Lost and Damned features a car based on the AMC Pacer named "Rhapsody" in reference to the famed scene from the film. Interestingly if one zooms in on the dashboard with the sniper rifle, they can see a photograph of Wayne and Garth.

Music

- The use of Queen's "Bohemian Rhapsody" in the film propelled the song to #2 in *Billboard* singles charts nearly 20 years after its first release. The soundtrack album reached number one in the *Billboard* album charts. Freddie Mercury, the lead singer of Queen, died of AIDS just a few months before the film's release.
- Joan Jett & the Blackhearts played again its famous theme "I Love Rock 'n' Roll" for the movie, with a new music video. The song reached the most places in the Billboards charts 10 years after of its release.Wikipedia:Please clarify
- Gary Wright rerecorded "Dream Weaver" for this film and it was used whenever Wayne looked at Cassandra.
- While in the music store, Wayne (Myers) tries out a guitar by starting to play "Stairway to Heaven" by Led Zeppelin, and is stopped by a salesman (often falsely credited as Dana Strum from the band Slaughter), who points to a sign on the wall of the sales floor, which says "No Stairway". This performance existed in original 35mm theatrical prints, but, due to the band's licensing restrictions, the notes performed were changed for home video and television broadcasts and bear no resemblance to the original, and the point of the joke is lost. Also, when Garth (Carvey) tries out a large Yamaha drum kit, the scene as filmed was actually Carvey playing the drum kit (microphones can be seen mounted on the kit to record the performance). Carvey had played drums during appearances as The Church Lady on *Saturday Night Live*.
- Tia Carrere sang all her own vocals on songs she performed in the film, and were included in the film's original soundtrack recording.

See also

- 1992 in film
- Recurring Saturday Night Live characters and sketches
- List of Saturday Night Live feature films

External links

- *Wayne's World* [1] at the Internet Movie Database
- *Wayne's World* [2] at Allmovie
- *Wayne's World* [3] at Rotten Tomatoes

Tommy Boy

Tommy Boy	
Tommy Boy Movie Poster	
Directed by	Peter Segal
Produced by	Lorne Michaels
Written by	Bonnie Turner Terry Turner Fred Wolf (uncredited)
Starring	Chris Farley David Spade Bo Derek Julie Warner with Dan Aykroyd and Brian Dennehy uncredited: Rob Lowe
Music by	David Newman
Cinematography	Victor J. Kemper
Editing by	William Kerr
Distributed by	Paramount Pictures
Release date(s)	March 31, 1995
Running time	97 min.
Language	English

Tommy Boy is a 1995 comedy film directed by Peter Segal, written by Bonnie and Terry Turner, and Fred Wolf, and starring former *Saturday Night Live* colleagues Chris Farley and David Spade. The main plot tells a story of the title character (portrayed by Farley), a socially and emotionally immature man who learns lessons about friendship, trust and self-worth following the sudden death of his industrialist father. The film did well commercially, but on average was not favored by film critics.[*citation needed*]

Plot

At Marquette University, Thomas R. "Tommy Boy" Callahan III (Chris Farley) barely graduates after seven years and returns home to Sandusky, Ohio. His proud father, industrialist Tom Callahan Sr. (Brian Dennehy), gives him an executive job at the family's auto parts plant, Callahan Auto.

In addition to a job and an office, Tom Sr. reveals other surprises for his son: Tom Sr. is engaged to a woman he met at a fat farm, Beverly Barish-Burns (Bo Derek), and that Tommy will soon have a stepbrother, Beverly's son Paul (Rob Lowe). But, Tom Sr. suffers a fatal heart attack during the wedding reception. At a board meeting after the funeral, the bank reneges on loans Tom Sr. had negotiated to pay for a new brake pad division, which he thought would be the future of the company.

Fearing the demise of his family's company, Tommy comes up with an idea: Give the bank his inheritance as collateral and then go on a cross-nation sales trip with his father's former assistant, Richard Hayden (David Spade). Tommy and Richard, a childhood friend who is greatly jealous of Tommy's ability to be lazy and yet be rewarded, hit the road in a last-ditch effort to save the company by selling 500,000 brake pads. They take off in Richard's prized 1967 Plymouth GTX convertible, which is eventually destroyed during a series of mishaps.

Meanwhile, Beverly and Paul are shown kissing romantically at a fair. They are not mother and son, but a married couple of con artists with criminal records. Their plan to steal from Tom Sr. has paid off early. Instead of eventually suing for divorce and taking half of Tom Senior's estate, Beverly has inherited half the company and she seeks a quick sale to self-described "auto parts king" Ray Zalinsky (Dan Aykroyd).

On the road, Tommy's comical social awkwardness, hyperactivity and inexperience alienate several potential buyers. These failures lead to friction between Tommy and Richard and eventually leads to a fight between the two. But, later at a restaurant, Tommy uses his innate persuasive powers to convince a surly waitress to serve him after the kitchen closed, showing his potential. The pair make sales and mend their fraying friendship. They soon reach their sales quota.

However, Paul sabotages the company's computers. Sales posted by sales manager Michelle Brock (Julie Warner) are either lost or rerouted. Tommy and Richard also are informed that half of the orders were cancelled since some of Callahan's buyers were not convinced of the company's new product. The eve of the sale to Zalinsky arrives and the top employees of the company head over to Chicago to transfer control of the company to Zalinsky, who plans to shut down the company, lay off the 300 employees who work there, and keep the company name for himself. Because Tommy already gave his share of the company's inheritance to the bank he is excluded from participating in the meeting. However, Tommy and Richard decide to travel to Chicago to persuade Zalinsky to not buy the company the night before the meeting occurs as the two seem optimistic that they can make him reconsider.

Initially, Tommy and Richard are kicked out of the board room because Tommy has no standing. As the pair wallow on the curb in self-pity, Michelle arrives with police records proving that Paul and Beverly are married con artists.

Tommy devises a 'plan:' Taking road flares from a nearby construction site, Tommy dresses himself as a bogus suicide bomber and forces his way back into the board room. His antics attract a live news TV camera crew which films the scene. In Sandusky, Callahan workers watch the drama unfold via a conveniently placed television.

Tommy reveals his deception, but quotes the auto king's own advertising claim of being on the side of "the American working man".[citation needed] As a TV audience watches, Zalinsky signs a purchase order for the one-half million brake pads. Workers in Sandusky cheer. The TV crew, having obtained what they thought was a dramatic conclusion to their story, leave the scene.

Then, Zalinsky says that the purchase order is meaningless as he will soon own Callahan Auto. However, Michelle shows her police documents, which includes Paul's outstanding warrants for three different counts of fraud: A Mail fraud count in New Mexico, a Wire fraud count in Colorado, and a Computer fraud relating to his tampering with the plant's computer the day before. The group around the table works through the logic together: Beverly was married to Paul when she married Tom Sr. Therefore, the marriage was invalid, and thus, Beverly could not inherit control of the company. The shares actually belong to Tommy.

Tommy says he doesn't want to sell, so the deal with Zalinsky is off. Tommy still holds Zalinsky's purchase order, meaning that he has saved the company which he now controls. Paul, furious with the results, attempts to escape but is arrested. Beverly goes to dinner with Zalinsky and Tommy is introduced as the new president of Callahan Auto, Inc.

Cast

- Chris Farley as Thomas "Tommy" Callahan III
- David Spade as Richard Hayden
- Rob Lowe as Paul Barrish
- Bo Derek as Beverly Barrish
- Dan Aykroyd as Ray Zalinsky
- Brian Dennehy as Thomas "Big Tom" Callahan Jr.
- Julie Warner as Michelle Brock
- William Patterson Dunlop as R.T.
- Ron James as Bank Security guard

Reception

Tommy Boy opened as the No. 1 movie in the United States on March 31, 1995, eventually falling out of the Top 20 within seven weeks. Total U.S. box office gross was $32,648,673.

The film did well financially, but received mixed reviews from critics upon its initial release. Rotten Tomatoes' index rates the film at 45%. *Chicago Sun-Times* film critic Roger Ebert wrote: "No one is funny in *Tommy Boy*. There are no memorable lines. None of the characters are interesting except for the enigmatic figure played by Rob Lowe, who seems to have wandered over from *Hamlet*." The *New York Times'* Caryn James said the film was "the very poor cousin of a dopey Jim Carrey movie".

The film received positive reviews from the *Lawrence Journal-World*, the *Los Angeles Times*, and the *Arizona Daily Star*. Since its release, some critics have suggested the film is a "cult classic".

Soundtrack

Warner Brothers soundtrack release

1. "I Love It Loud (Injected Mix)" - written by Gene Simmons & Vincent Cusano, performed by Phunk Junkeez
2. Graduation - David Spade
3. "Silver Naked Ladies" - Paul Westerberg
4. Lalaluukee - David Spade
5. "Call On Me" - Primal Scream
6. How Do I Look? - David Spade
7. "Wait For The Blackout" - written by The Damned (Scabies/Sensible/Gray/Vanian/Billy Karloff), performed by The Goo Goo Dolls
8. Bong Resin - David Spade
9. "My Hallucination" - Tommy Shaw & Jack Blades
10. "Air" - written by Pamela Laws & Nancy Hess, performed by Seven Day Diary
11. Fat Guy In Little Coat - Chris Farley
12. "Superstar" - written by Leon Russell , Delaney Bramlett, & Bonnie Bramlett, performed by The Carpenters
13. Jerk Motel - David Spade
14. "Is Chicago, Is Not Chicago" - Soul Coughing
15. My Pretty Little Pet - Cris Farley
16. "Come On Eileen" - Dexys Midnight Runners
17. It's the End of the World as We Know It (And I Feel Fine) - R.E.M.
18. "Eres Tú" - written by Juan Carlos Calderón, performed by Mocedades
19. Housekeeping - David Spade
20. "My Lucky Day" - Smoking Popes

21. Poop - David Spade

Other songs

1. "What'd I Say" - written by Ray Charles, performed by Chris Farley and Brian Dennehy
2. "Maniac" - written by Michael Sembello and Dennis Matkosky
3. "Ain't Too Proud To Beg" - written by Eddie Holland & Norman Whitfield, performed by Louis Price
4. "Amazing Grace" - performed by The Pipes and Drums and Military of The King's Own Scottish Borderers
5. "Crazy" - written by Willie Nelson, performed by Patsy Cline
6. "I'm Sorry" - written by Ronnie Self & Dub Allbritten, performed by Brenda Lee
7. "Ooh Wow" - written by Sidney Cooper, performed by Buckwheat Zydeco
8. "The Future's So Bright, I Gotta Wear Shades" - written by Pat MacDonald, performed by Timbuk 3
9. "The Merry-Go-Round Broke Down" - Cliff Friend & Dave Franklin

External links

- *Tommy Boy* [1] at the Internet Movie Database
- *Tommy Boy* [2] at Allmovie

Brain Candy

Brain Candy	
Directed by	Kelly Makin
Produced by	Lorne Michaels
Written by	Kevin McDonald Scott Thompson Mark McKinney Bruce McCulloch Norm Hiscock
Starring	Kevin McDonald Scott Thompson Mark McKinney Bruce McCulloch Dave Foley
Distributed by	Paramount Pictures

Release date(s)	April 12, 1996 (US) November 8, 1996 (UK) March 12, 1997 (France)
Running time	89 minutes
Language	English

Brain Candy (aka ***Kids in the Hall: Brain Candy***) is a feature film by The Kids in the Hall, a Canadian comedy troupe. Directed by Kelly Makin, filmed in Toronto, and released in 1996, it followed the five season run of their television series, which had been successful in both Canada and the United States.

The five man team plays all of the major characters, and many of the bit parts. Brendan Fraser and Janeane Garofalo have cameos, Garofalo's being almost entirely absent from the final cut. The film has since become a cult classic.

Premise and characters

The film is about the introduction of a powerful antidepressant, GLeeMONEX. The drug is rushed into production to help the ailing Roritor Pharmaceuticals and becomes an overnight media sensation. Those involved in the early stages of GLeeMONEX- the scientists, marketing arm and several early users - are followed, right up through the troubling coma-like side effect of being stuck in their happiest memory.

- **Chris Cooper** (Kevin McDonald) is the inventor of the drug, and main protagonist of the film. He is motivated by the clumsy suicide of his father (also played by McDonald) to create a cure for clinical depression, but quickly gets swept up in the resulting fame.
- **Alice** (Bruce McCulloch) is a fellow scientist, and apparent love interest of Chris. She eventually watches from a distance as he slips away into celebrity.
- **Don Roritor** (Mark McKinney) heads Roritor Pharmaceuticals, founded on his invention of the drug Stummies (likely a play on Tums or Rolaids). He has a close but contentious relationship with his spineless assistant, Marv. (Roritor's speaking style is openly derived from McKinney's notorious impersonations of producer Lorne Michaels.)
- **Marv** (Dave Foley) is Roritor's assistant. Despite their seemingly close relationship, he actually dislikes Roritor to the point that his happiest memory is having someone urinate in his boss' latte (Roritor's happiest moment, ironically, is drinking the concoction).
- **Mrs. Hurdicure** (Scott Thompson) is an old woman who initially is severely depressed and an early test subject for GLeeMONEX (referred to as "Patient 957"). Her happiest memory is shown to be a brief and obligatory Christmas visit from her son, played by Dave Foley. The drug quickly whips her out of the depression, but she inevitably becomes the first victim of its side effect.
- **Wally Terzinsky** (Scott Thompson) is a husband, father, and closeted homosexual. Wally masturbates to gay pornography, frequents public bath houses, and was sexually active with men

during his military career - but remains unaware of his sexual orientation. He is prescribed GLeeMONEX by a frustrated therapist, played by Dave Foley ("You're gay. I know it, your family knows it... *dogs* know it!"). His happiest memory is a homoerotic army mission fantasized by Wally while being chewed out by his drill sergeant (played by Mark McKinney). Wally finds himself standing considerably closer to his drill sergeant when through fantasizing. Shortly after this, he finally admits (via song and dance) that he is in fact homosexual. The character is an obvious variation on the TV show's dimwitted Danny Husk (even featuring Kevin McDonald as his wife in both the movie and series).

- **Grivo** (Bruce McCulloch) is a rock star (evidently a parody of Glenn Danzig) famous for his bleak lyrics, as well as a general indifference toward his audience, fame, and music. After taking the drug, Grivo switches to jangly, upbeat pop music; his song "Happiness Pie" becomes an anthem for the post-GLeeMONEX world and wins an MTV Video Award for Best New Video.

Some characters from the television series appear briefly in *Brain Candy*. Among those who do are the "white trash couple," the cops, Cancer Boy (see below), talk show host Nina Bedford (introduced in the show as "Nina Spudkneeyak"), Raj & Lacey, Melanie, Bellini, and the bigoted cab driver (who narrates the film).

Controversy

Two of the film's characters created minor waves in the media before its release. The first was Don Roritor, which many took to be a jab at producer Lorne Michaels. Michaels is famous for creating Saturday Night Live, and was responsible for bringing the Kids in the Hall to television. He is also known for a demeanor that some interpret as detached, and Mark McKinney mirrors his speech patterns almost exactly as the cold-hearted Roritor.

The second contentious character was Cancer Boy. Reprised from the final episode of the TV show, in a sketch that satirized the idea of being as offensive as possible, Cancer Boy is Bruce McCulloch dressed in a bald cap, with pale white makeup, and confined to a wheelchair. He relays depressing information with a cheerful smile and releases a hit pop single entitled "Whistle When You're Low." Many found the character to be in exceedingly poor taste. Paramount Pictures fought extensively with the troupe to cut the offending scenes, to no avail. The group has expressed some regret over their hardline position years later, feeling the battle left Paramount bitter and reluctant to fully market the film.

Reaction

The film opened to a lukewarm critical reception. Siskel and Ebert were split, and had a heated disagreement over *Brain Candy* on their weekly review show: Gene Siskel found the movie "audacious, clever, very funny" and predicted it would become a midnight cult film; Roger Ebert claimed that he did not laugh once during the screening and found it "awful, terrible, dreadful, stupid, idiotic, unfunny, labored, forced, painful, bad." Janet Maslin of *The New York Times* called it "[nothing] more than a sloppy showcase for the group's costume-changing tricks." Edward Guthmann at *The San Francisco Chronicle*, however, called *Brain Candy* "a splendid showcase for their diverse, frisky talents." It maintains a 41 percent rating on Rotten Tomatoes.

The film suffered poor box office returns. The Kids themselves have expressed mixed feelings over the finished product, most notably on the behind-the-scenes DVD of their 2000 tour, *Same Guys, New Dresses*. The troupe took a four year hiatus after *Brain Candy* 's release, though the break-up was already in motion even before filming was underway.

Alternate title and ending

An original working title for the movie was *The Drug*, which is what GLeeMONEX is extensively referred to during the course of the film (in fact, "Brain Candy" is never actually heard in the film). Bruce McCulloch came up with *Brain Candy* at the studio's request for something more marketable.

Two endings were filmed, with the relatively more upbeat conclusion making the final cut. In the alternate version, Dave Foley plays a crazed activist who leads a militant movement against GLeeMONEX. Chris Cooper, unable to cope with the mayhem his drug has created, decides to take it himself, and ends up lapsing into a coma. The unused ending has not been officially released, but a leaked work print was widely traded among fans on the internet during the late 1990s.

Soundtrack

Brain Candy - Music From The Motion Picture Soundtrack	
Soundtrack	
Released	1996-04-09
Genre	Movie Soundtrack
Length	52:28
Label	Matador Records
Professional reviews	
• Allmusic ★ ★ ★ ★ link [1]	

A soundtrack album was released the Tuesday prior to the film's release. It consists of music from the film, interspersed with dialog.

Track List

1. "Some Days It's Dark" - Death Lurks (McCulloch as Grivo with Odds) (with film dialog)
2. "Painted Soldiers" - Pavement
3. "Happiness" - Matthew Sweet
4. "Happiness Pie" - Death Lurks
5. "Six Dick Pimp" - Liz Phair (followed by dialog leading into next track)
6. "I'm Gay" - Scott Thompson and Joe Sealy
7. "Spiralling Shape" - They Might Be Giants
8. "Swoon" - Pell Mell
9. "Birthday Cake" - Cibo Matto
10. "Butts Wigglin" - The Tragically Hip
11. "Postal Blowfish" - Guided By Voices
12. "Pablo And Andrea" - Yo La Tengo
13. "How To Play Your Internal Organs Overnight!" - Stereolab
14. "Nata Di Marzo" - Pizzicato Five
15. "Eat My Brain" - Odds
16. "Long Dark Twenties" - Paul Bellini
17. "Having an Average Weekend" - Shadowy Men on a Shadowy Planet

External links

- *Kids in the Hall: Brain Candy* [2] at the Internet Movie Database
- Bruce McCulloch as Cancer Boy [3]
- Original 1996 Film Review [4] from Ebert and Roeper (video clip)

A Night at the Roxbury

A Night at the Roxbury	
Theatrical poster	
Directed by	John Fortenberry
Produced by	Amy Heckerling Lorne Michaels
Written by	Will Ferrell Chris Kattan
Starring	Will Ferrell Chris Kattan Molly Shannon Loni Anderson Dan Hedaya
Music by	David Kitay
Cinematography	Francis Kenny
Editing by	Jay Kamen
Studio	SNL Studios
Distributed by	Paramount Pictures United International Pictures
Release date(s)	October 2, 1998
Running time	81 minutes
Country	
Language	English
Budget	$17,000,000 (estimated)
Gross revenue	$30,331,165

A Night at the Roxbury is a 1998 comedy film based on a recurring skit on television's long-running *Saturday Night Live* called "The Roxbury Guys." *Saturday Night Live* regulars Will Ferrell, Chris Kattan, Molly Shannon, and Colin Quinn star.

The film sees Kattan and Ferrell reprise their *SNL* characters, dense nightclubbing brothers Doug and Steve Butabi. In the original sketches, Doug and Steve were often joined by that night's guest, credited as 'barhop' (including turns by Jim Carrey, Tom Hanks, Martin Short, Alec Baldwin, Jack Nicholson, and Sylvester Stallone parodying his familiar Rocky Balboa role), but the barhop role was dropped during production of the film.

Other roles include Jennifer Coolidge as a police officer, Chazz Palminteri's uncredited role as gregarious night club impresario Mr. Benny Zadir, and Colin Quinn as his bodyguard. Ex-*SNL*er Mark McKinney has a cameo as a priest officiating a wedding.

Plot

Wearing rayon suits, Speedo trunks, hair gel and cologne, wealthy Yemenite-American brothers Steve (Will Ferrell) and Doug Butabi (Chris Kattan) enjoy frequenting nightclubs, where they bob their heads in unison to dance music (specifically Haddaway's hit song "What Is Love") and fail miserably at picking up women. Their dream is to party at the Roxbury, a fabled nightclub where they are continually denied entrance by a hulking bouncer (Michael Clarke Duncan).

By day, the brothers work at a fake-plant store owned by their wealthy father, Kamehl Butabi (Dan Hedaya). They spend most of their time goofing off, daydreaming about opening a club as cool as the Roxbury together, and Doug uses credit card transactions as an excuse to hit on a phone approval operator. They also have an annoying habit of overenthusiastically retelling to everyone they stand in line with their story of how they met Emilio Estevez while waiting in line to use a payphone. Also not amusing to anyone but themselves is a supposed joke in which they "trick" a questioner by answering, "No" before switching to their "real" answer, "Yes." Walking down to their father's store, to the beat of "Stayin Alive", they try to pick a girl (Gina Mari) walking toward them, only to get beaten up by her.

The store shares a wall with a lighting emporium owned by Fred Sanderson (Dwayne Hickman of Dobie Gillis fame). Both Mr. Butabi and Mr. Sanderson hope that Steve and Emily (Molly Shannon), Sanderson's daughter, will marry, uniting the families and the businesses to form the first plant-lamp emporium.

After a day at the beach, in which the Doug and Steve try to pick up women while wearing matching thongs, the brothers decide that tonight is the night they will finally get into the Roxbury. Returning home to the gauchely decorated bedroom they share, Doug, still wearing the same outfit as at the beach, gets into a heated argument with their father about going out clubbing instead of staying home. (Their father has planned a dinner party with Emily and her parents.) The angered Mr. Butabi then denies them access to their BMW car and to their cell phones. Given enormous cell phones by their mother (Loni Anderson) and allowed use of the fake-plant store's delivery van they are quickly rejected by the doorman (Michael Clarke Duncan). After discovering they might bribe their way into the club, the brothers drive around looking for an ATM. They get into a fender-bender with Richard Grieco (playing himself) and, to avoid a lawsuit, Grieco uses his fame to get them into the popular club. There they meet the owner of the Roxbury, Benny Zadir (Chazz Palminteri), who listens to their ideas for a nightclub of their own. He likes them and sets up a meeting with them for the next day. The brothers also meet a pair of women at the Roxbury: Vivica (Gigi Rice) and Cambi (Elisa Donovan), who see them talking to Zadir and think that the brothers are rich.

On the way to the after party at Mr. Zadir's house the brothers annoy his driver and bodyguard Dooey (Colin Quinn) by making him stop to buy fluffy whip and making jokes about sleeping with his mother. As revenge, the next day Dooey denies them entry into Zadir's office for their meeting. He tells the brothers that Zadir was drunk out of his mind last night and doesn't know who they are, though Zadir really does want to see them (but does not have their contact information). Afterwards, the girls break up with the Butabi brothers after realizing they're not really wealthy. The brothers fight and Doug moves out of their shared bedroom and into the guest house. Meanwhile Steve is forced into an engagement with the Sandersons' daughter, Emily. The wedding is held in the backyard of the Butabi residence, but is interrupted by Doug: Having gone on a fluffy-whip-fueled bender, he stands atop the guest house staircase with a boom-box blasting the song "What Is Love" (an allusion to the movie Say Anything).

As Doug begins bobbing his head, Steve cannot help but mimic his brother, a sign that he is beginning to remember what he really wants and who he truly is. Steve breaks off the marriage to Emily and departs. In an act of desperation, Steve's former personal trainer/friend/best man Craig (Lochlyn Munro) opts to marry Emily, admitting his longtime crush on her. Emily agrees to marry Craig as long as he promises to invest in infomercials and protein bars. Meanwhile, Richard Grieco (a guest at the wedding) talks to Mr. Butabi to help him understand that Steve was not ready for marriage, and that Butabi is too hard on Doug. The brothers forgive each other and then proceed to go clubbing in their new colored suits.

The movie ends as the Butabi brothers happen upon a hot new club opened by Zadir. The building is unique in that the exterior is constructed to resemble the interior of a nightclub, and the interior resembles a street — this was an idea pitched by Doug and Steve earlier in the movie. Attempting to enter, they are surprised to find their names on the VIP list. In addition, Zadir reveals that to reward their idea, he has made them part-owners of the club. Their new-found success comes full circle when they meet another two women in the club: Doug's phone representative from the credit card company (Meredith Scott Lynn) and a police officer (Jennifer Coolidge) whom Steve earlier flirted with while getting a ticket. Out on the dance floor, Doug, Steve, and the two women begin to bob their heads in unison to "What Is Love," and all the other nightclub patrons do the same.

Cast

- Chris Kattan as Doug Butabi
- Will Ferrell as Steve Butabi
- Loni Anderson as Barbara Butabi
- Dan Hedaya as Kamehl Butabi
- Molly Shannon as Emily Sanderson
- Dwayne Hickman as Fred Sanderson
- Maree Cheatham as Mabel Sanderson

- Lochlyn Munro as Craig
- Richard Grieco as Himself
- Jennifer Coolidge as Hottie Police Officer
- Meredith Scott Lynn as Credit Vixen
- Elisa Donovan as Cambi
- Gigi Rice as Vivica
- Colin Quinn as Dooey
- Twink Caplan as Crying Flower Customer
- Eva Mendes as Bridesmaid
- Mark McKinney as Father Williams
- Michael Clarke Duncan as the Roxbury Bouncer
- Chazz Palminteri as Benny Zadir (uncredited)
- Christian Mixon as Guy In Corvette
- Rachel Galvin as a girl on the beach

Reception

The film was universally panned by critics, garnering an 11% Rating on Rotten Tomatoes with the consensus that "*A Night at the Roxbury* suffers from what every SNL movie has: a stupid plot, poor acting, and terrible dialogue." Roger Ebert gave the film an abysmal score of half a star out of four, saying, "The movie is a mess. It is incompetent, stupid, and horrible beyond belief. It sucks on so many levels." Despite these ratings, the film has gained a cult following, and its theme song, "What Is Love," has become a part of mainstream American culture.

Soundtrack

1. "What Is Love" - Haddaway
2. "Bamboogie (Radio Edit)" - Bamboo
3. "Make That Money (Roxbury Remix)" - Robi Rob's Club World
4. "Disco Inferno" - Cyndi Lauper
5. "Do Ya Think I'm Sexy" - N-Trance featuring Rod Stewart
6. "Pop Muzik" - 3rd Party
7. "Insomnia (Monster Mix)" - Faithless
8. "Be My Lover (Club Mix)" - La Bouche
9. "This Is Your Night" - Amber
10. "Beautiful Life" - Ace of Base
11. "Where Do You Go (Ocean Drive Mix)" - No Mercy
12. "A Little Bit of Ecstasy" - Jocelyn Enriquez
13. "What is Love? (Refreshmento Extro Radio Mix)" - Haddaway

14. "Careless Whisper" - Tamia
15. "Secret Garden" - Bruce Springsteen
16. "Everybody Hurts" - R.E.M.

External links

- *A Night at the Roxbury* [1] at the Internet Movie Database
- *A Night at the Roxbury* [2] at the TCM Movie Database
- *A Night at the Roxbury* [3] at Allmovie

Mean Girls

Mean Girls	
Theatrical release poster	
Directed by	Mark Waters
Produced by	Lorne Michaels Tony Shimkin Louise Rosner Jill Messick
Written by	Tina Fey **Book:** Rosalind Wiseman
Starring	Lindsay Lohan Rachel McAdams Lacey Chabert Amanda Seyfried Tina Fey
Music by	Rolfe Kent
Cinematography	Daryn Okada
Editing by	Wendy Greene Bricmont
Distributed by	Paramount Pictures
Release date(s)	April 30, 2004
Running time	96 minutes
Country	United States Canada

Language	English German Vietnamese Swahili
Budget	$17 million
Gross revenue	$129,042,871
Followed by	*Mean Girls 2*

Mean Girls is a 2004 American/Canadian teen comedy film, directed by Mark Waters. The screenplay was written by Tina Fey and based in part on the non-fiction book *Queen Bees and Wannabes* by Rosalind Wiseman, which describes how female high school social cliques operate, and the effect they can have on girls. The film stars Lindsay Lohan and features a supporting cast of Rachel McAdams, Amanda Seyfried, Lacey Chabert, and Lizzy Caplan. The film also features several *Saturday Night Live* cast members, including Tina Fey, Tim Meadows, Ana Gasteyer, and Amy Poehler.

Described by director Mark Waters as "*Clueless* meets *Heathers*", *Mean Girls* follows the home-schooled 16-year-old Cady Heron (Lohan) as she enters her first year of public high school.

The film was generally well received by critics and was a big financial success, grossing $129,042,871 worldwide. *Mean Girls* has been praised as Lohan's break-out film role. A sequel, *Mean Girls 2*, is currently in production. *Mean Moms*, a quasi-spinoff, based on Wiseman's second book, *Queen Bees Moms & King Pin Dads*, is also in development.

Plot

The 16-year-old home-schooled daughter of zoologist parents (Ana Gasteyer and Neil Flynn) living somewhere in East Africa, Cady Heron (Lindsay Lohan), is unprepared for her first day of public high school at fictional North Shore High School in Evanston, Illinois. With the help of social outcasts Janis (Lizzy Caplan) and Damien (Daniel Franzese), Cady learns about the various cliques. She is warned to avoid the school's most exclusive clique, the Plastics, the reigning trio of girls led by the acid-tongued queen bee Regina George (Rachel McAdams). Regina was once Janis's best friend but they have grown to despise each other since Regina started a rumor about Janis's sexuality in 8th grade. However, the Plastics take a shine to Cady and invite her to sit with them at lunch and go shopping with them after school.

After realizing that Cady has been accepted into the Plastics, Janis hatches a plan to get revenge on Regina for what she did to her, using Cady as a pawn in order to infiltrate the Plastics. Cady supports her after Regina mistreats her at a Halloween party. Janis's plan involves cutting off Regina's "resources", which include separating her from her boyfriend Aaron Samuels (Jonathan Bennett), destroying her beauty, and turning Regina's fellow Plastics against her: insecure rich girl Gretchen

Wieners (Lacey Chabert) and sweet but dimwitted Karen Smith (Amanda Seyfried).

Having ingratiated herself with the Plastics per Janis's plan, Cady learns about the "Burn Book," a top secret notebook of Regina's filled with slandering rumors, secrets, and gossip about all the other girls (and teachers) in their class. Cady soon falls in love with Aaron, whom Regina successfully steals back from Cady in a fit of jealousy. Cady then ups the ante by pretending failure at math to get Aaron's attention, and in retaliation against Regina, convincing the latter to eat high-calorie nutrition bars by claiming that they actually help one *lose* weight. She also choreographs Aaron's breakup with Regina by confessing Regina's infidelity with another boy.

In her efforts to get revenge on Regina, Cady gradually loses her individual personality and remakes herself in the image of Regina. Her act soon becomes reality, and she becomes as spiteful as Regina, abandoning Janis and Damien in the process and focusing more on her image. Regina, now slightly overweight due to Cady's diet sabotage, is excluded from the Plastics and Cady becomes the new Queen Bee. In celebration of her newfound status, Cady throws a party with the Plastics and does not invite Janis or Damien. Janis and Damien then renounce Cady as a friend. During the party, she also alienates Aaron with her unsavory new personality.

Regina discovers the truth about the bars she has been eating and strikes back by spreading the entire contents of her Burn Book around the school, inciting a riot; to avoid suspicion, Regina also inserts fake slander of herself in the book, in order to focus blame on Cady, Gretchen, and Karen. The riot is eventually quelled by Principal Duvall (Tim Meadows). Math teacher Ms. Norbury (Tina Fey)—who also appeared in the Burn Book, where Cady slandered her by saying that she sold drugs—makes the girls realize that all of them are guilty of hurting their peers. She has each girl confess and apologize to the rest of the girls. Janis confesses her plan to destroy Regina with Cady's help, and openly mocks Regina with the support of the entire school. Regina storms out, pursued by an apologetic Cady, and gets hit by a school bus in her haste; rumors circulate that Cady intentionally pushed Regina in front of the bus.

Now without friends, shunned by Aaron, and distrusted by everyone at school, Cady decides to make amends by taking full blame for the Burn Book. Though severely punished by her confession, her guilt dissolves and she returns to her old personality. As punishment for her part, Ms. Norbury has Cady join the Mathletes—which Damien & Regina both described earlier as "social suicide"—in their competition.

At the Spring Fling dance, Cady is elected Spring Fling Queen and gives a speech to her class that her victory is meaningless; they are all wonderful in their own way and thus the victory belongs to everyone. As a symbolic gesture, she breaks her tiara and distributes the pieces to her fellow classmates. Cady makes up with Janis and Damien, reconciles with Aaron, and reaches a truce with the Plastics.

The film ends with the Plastics disbanding by the start of the new school year: Regina joins the lacrosse team as a way to channel her anger positively, Karen becomes the school weather girl (claiming that her breasts can always tell when it's raining), Gretchen joins the "Cool Asians" clique and is their biggest follower, and Cady dates Aaron as well as hanging out with Janis and Damien. Now reasonably well-liked, Cady reflects that the "Girl World" she lives in is at peace.

Cast

- Lindsay Lohan as Cady Heron
- Rachel McAdams as Regina George
- Lacey Chabert as Gretchen Weiners
- Amanda Seyfried as Karen Smith
- Tina Fey as Ms. Sharon Norbury
- Tim Meadows as Principal Ron Duvall
- Jonathan Bennett as Aaron Samuels
- Lizzy Caplan as Janis Ian; Fey has said that while writing the film she kept referring to this character as "this Janis Ian type" because of the singer's song "At Seventeen" (which also appears in the film). She eventually decided to just name the character "Janis Ian".
- Daniel Franzese as Damien
- Amy Poehler as Mrs. George
- Ana Gasteyer as Betsy Heron
- Neil Flynn as Chip Heron
- Rajiv Surendra as Kevin Gnapoor
- Diego Klattenhoff as Shane Oman

Production

Though set on the North Shore of Chicago, the film was partly shot in Toronto, Ontario, Canada at Etobicoke Collegiate Institute and Malvern Collegiate Institute.[*citation needed*] Notable landmarks include the University of Toronto's Convocation Hall and Sherway Gardens. Regina George's house is a home in the Bridle Path neighborhood.[*citation needed*]

Reception

The film was generally well reviewed by critics, review aggregator website Rotten Tomatoes gave it a rating of 83% "Fresh" based on 167 reviews. and a rating of 66 ("Generally favorable reviews") on Metacritic based on 39 reviews.

The film was declared an instant success after its opening weekend made $24,432,195 from 2,839 theaters becoming the #1 film in America and averaging $8,606 per venue. *Mean Girls* had a long life at the box office and finished its run with $86,058,055 in the United States making its worldwide total gross $129,042,871. In the US, the film was the 24th highest grossing film of 2004.

In an interview about the film, Tina Fey noted, "Adults find it funny. They are the ones who are laughing. Young people watch it like a reality television show. It is much too close to their real experiences so they are not exactly guffawing." *Entertainment Weekly* put it on its end-of-the-decade, "best-of" list, saying, " "Fetch" may never happen, but 2004's eminently quotable movie is still one of the sharpest high school satires ever. Which is pretty grool, if you ask us." In 2006, Entertainment Weekly also named it the 12th best high school movie of all times, explaining: "There was a time when Lindsay Lohan was best known for her acting rather than her party-hopping. Showcasing La Lohan in arguably her best role to date, this Tina Fey-scripted film also boasts a breakout turn by Rachel McAdams as evil queen bee Regina George (*Gretchen, stop trying to make 'fetch' happen! It's not going to happen!*). While Mean Girls is technically a comedy, its depiction of girl-on-girl cattiness stings incredibly true."

Awards

The film received many award wins and nominations. The film was nominated for 13 Teen Choice Awards, winning four. The film was also nominated for four MTV Movie Awards, winning three of them. The film was nominated for the WGA Award for Best Adapted Screenplay.

Year	Ceremony	Award	Result
2004	Teen Choice Awards	Choice Movie Comedy Actress: Lindsay Lohan	Won
2004	Teen Choice Awards	Choice Movie Breakout Actress: Lindsay Lohan	Won
2004	Teen Choice Awards	Choice Hissy Fit	Won
2004	Teen Choice Awards	Choice Movie Blush: Lindsay Lohan	Won
2004	Teen Choice Awards	Choice Breakout Movie Star - Female: Rachel McAdams	Nominated
2004	Teen Choice Awards	Choice Breakout Movie Star - Male: Jonathan Bennett	Nominated
2004	Teen Choice Awards	Choice Movie - Comedy	Nominated
2004	Teen Choice Awards	Choice Movie Actress - Comedy: Rachel McAdams	Nominated
2004	Teen Choice Awards	Choice Movie Blush: Rachel McAdams	Nominated
2004	Teen Choice Awards	Choice Movie Chemistry: Lindsay Lohan Jonathan Bennett	Nominated
2004	Teen Choice Awards	Choice Movie Fight/Action Sequence	Nominated

2004	Teen Choice Awards	Choice Movie Hissy Fit: Rachel McAdams	Nominated
2004	Teen Choice Awards	Choice Movie Liar: Lindsay Lohan	Nominated
2004	Teen Choice Awards	Choice Movie Sleazebag: Rachel McAdams	Nominated
2005	MTV Movie Awards	Best Female Performance	Won
2005	MTV Movie Awards	Breakthrough Female Performance	Won
2005	MTV Movie Awards	Best On-Screen Team	Won
2005	MTV Movie Awards	Best Villain	Nominated
2005	Kids Choice Awards	Favorite Movie Actress	Nominated
2005	People's Choice Awards	Favorite Movie: Comedy	Nominated
2005	WGA Award	Best Adapted Screenplay: Tina Fey	Nominated

Influences on pop culture

- Pop/R&B singer Mariah Carey expressed several times that she's a fan of the film, using some quotes from the film in several interviews, most notably on *The Ellen Degeneres Show* in 2005 and in her official Twitter updates in 2009. Carey released the first single from her album *Memoirs of an Imperfect Angel*, called "Obsessed", which begins with an interlude quote where she says, "And I was like, 'Why are you so obsessed with me?'", a line said by Regina in the film. Carey's husband, Nick Cannon, debunked other theories and revealed the song was inspired by the film itself.
- Country singer Kellie Pickler, before Carey, used the accident scene in her 2008 single, "Best Days of Your Life".[citation needed]Wikipedia:Please clarify
- The film helped inspire the popular wrestling alliance, The Beautiful People.

References to other media

The scene immediately preceding the bus accident references *The Wizard of Oz*; the crowd raises up Janis, who is wearing black and white striped stockings similar to those worn by the Wicked Witch of the East, whose legs protruded from the house that killed her.

Soundtrack

Mean Girls	
Soundtrack by various artists	
Released	September 21, 2004
Genre	Rock, pop
Label	Rykodisc
Professional reviews	
• Allmusic ★★★★★ link [1]	

The soundtrack for the film was released on September 21, 2004, the same day as the DVD release.

Track listing

1. "Dancing with Myself" by The Donnas (Generation X cover)
2. "God Is a DJ" by Pink
3. "Milkshake" by Kelis
4. "Sorry (Don't Ask Me)" by All Too Much
5. "Built This Way" by Samantha Ronson
6. "Rip Her to Shreds" by Boomkat (Blondie cover)
7. "Overdrive" by Katy Rose
8. "One Way or Another" by Blondie
9. "Operate" by Peaches
10. "Misty Canyon" by Anjali Bhatia
11. "Mean Gurl" by Gina Rene and Gabriel Rene
12. "Hated" by Nikki Cleary
13. "Psyché Rock" by Pierre Henry
14. "The Mathlete Rap" by Rajiv Surendra

Though not included on the soundtrack, other songs heard in the film include "Pass That Dutch" by Missy Elliott, "Fire" by Joe Budden featuring Busta Rhymes, and "Halcyon + On + On" by Orbital.

Home media

The DVD was released in North America on September 21, 2004, five months after it opened in theaters. It was released in a widescreen special collector's edition and a fullscreen collector's edition, both including several deleted scenes, a blooper reel, three interstitials, the theatrical trailer, previews, and three featurettes. A Blu-ray version was released on April 14, 2009.

Video game

A video game for PC and Nintendo DS was released in 2009. The video game features characters specifically created for the game.

Sequel

See also: Mean Girls 2

A sequel to the film, *Mean Girls 2*, will be directed by Melanie Mayron. It was filmed in July 2010 in Atlanta. Maiara Walsh confirmed through her Twitter that she will star as the lead "Plastic" in the film. The story revolves around a new high school student Jo (Meaghan Jette Martin), who agrees to befriend an outcast, Abby (Jennifer Stone), at the urging of Abby's wealthy father in exchange for paying all of Jo's costs for the college of her dreams. Jo and Abby team up to take on the school's mean girls, the Plastics (Mandi, Hope, and Chasity) - Maiara Walsh, Nicole Anderson, and Claire Holt. The story becomes a high-stakes battle of loyalty that ultimately comes to a head when one of the heroines finds out that her friendship has been bought and paid for. Nicole Anderson (of *Jonas L.A.*) confirmed on her Twitter account that she will be in *Mean Girls 2* as did Jennifer Stone..

External links

- Official website [2]
- *Mean Girls* [3] at the Internet Movie Database
- *Mean Girls* [4] at Allmovie
- *Mean Girls* [5] at Box Office Mojo
- *Mean Girls* [6] at Rotten Tomatoes
- *Mean Girls* [7] at Metacritic

Baby Mama (film)

Baby Mama	
Theatrical release poster	
Directed by	Michael McCullers
Produced by	Lorne Michaels John Goldwyn
Written by	Michael McCullers
Starring	Tina Fey Amy Poehler Sigourney Weaver Greg Kinnear Dax Shepard
Music by	Jeff Richmond
Cinematography	Daryn Okada
Editing by	Bruce Green
Distributed by	Universal Pictures
Release date(s)	April 25, 2008
Running time	99 minutes
Country	United States
Language	English
Budget	$30 million
Gross revenue	$64,275,411

Baby Mama is a 2008 comedy film from Universal Pictures written and directed by Michael McCullers and starring Tina Fey, Amy Poehler, Sigourney Weaver, Greg Kinnear, and Dax Shepard.

Plot

Kate Holbrook (Tina Fey), a successful single businesswoman who attended The Wharton School from Philadelphia, has always put her career before her personal life. Now in her late thirties, she has finally decided to have a child on her own. Her plans change when she discovers she has only one in a millon chance of becoming pregnant because she finds out her uterus is T-shaped. Also denied the chance to adopt, Kate hires an immature, obnoxious South Philly girl named Angie Ostrowiski (Amy Poehler) to become her surrogate mother.

When Angie becomes pregnant, Kate begins preparing for motherhood in her own typically driven fashion — until her surrogate shows up at her door with no place to live. Their conflicting personalities put them at odds as Kate learns first-hand about balancing motherhood and career by catering to Angie's childish needs. As if this weren't enough, Kate begins dating the local owner of a blended juice cafe, Rob (Greg Kinnear).

What Kate does not know is that Angie is faking the pregnancy and that the in-vitro fertilization did not succeed. Hoping to ultimately run off with her payment, Angie begins to regret the lie but continually puts off confessing. When she gets an ultrasound, she discovers she is actually pregnant. Realizing the baby is her own (with her common-law husband, Carl, from whom she is separated), Angie is forced to confess at Kate's baby shower. When Kate explains to Angie that the pregnancy test was supposed to be taken two weeks after the procedure, and that the baby could still belong to her, it drives a wedge between the two women.

At the court hearing to determine the maternity of the child, Angie makes an impassioned apology. The baby turns out to be Angie's. Meeting face to face after the proceedings, Angie's water breaks and Kate rushes her to the hospital. During Angie's delivery, Kate passes out. Upon waking, the doctor supervising Angie's pregnancy tells Kate that she's three months pregnant (the result of her relationship with her new boyfriend). After receiving the news, she goes to visit Angie, who is holding her new baby girl Stefani, named for Gwen Stefani, aka "Stef." Kate forgives Angie and the two become best friends. Ultimately, changing eachother for the better.

Angie and Kate raise their children and are in a sister like relationship one year later at Stefani's first birthday party. It is revealed that Kate and Angie are best friends, and that Kate and Rob are very proud parents of a baby girl and engaged. Although he does not get back together with Angie, Carl stays close to his daughter and begins taking parenting classes.

Cast

- Tina Fey as Katherine "Kate" Holbrook
- Amy Poehler as Angela "Angie" Ostrowiski
- Greg Kinnear as Rob Ackerman
- Romany Malco as Oscar Priyan
- Dax Shepard as Carl Loomis
- Maura Tierney as Caroline Holbrook
- Steve Martin as Barry Waterman
- Sigourney Weaver as Chaffee Bicknell
- Holland Taylor as Rose Holbrook
- Stephen Mailer as Dan
- Siobhan Fallon Hogan as Birthing Teacher
- Kevin Collins as Rick

- Will Forte as Scott
- Denis O'Hare as Dr. Manheim
- Fred Armisen as Stroller Salesman
- James Rebhorn as Judge
- John Hodgman as Fertility Specialist
- Thomas McCarthy as Kate's Date (as Tom McCarthy)
- Jason Mantzoukas as Gay Couple
- Dave Finkel as Gay Couple
- Brian Stack as Dave
- Felicity Stiverson as Ashley - Wiccan
- Anne L. Nathan as Bookstore Clerk
- Jay Phillips as Boo-Boo Buster
- Kathy Searle as Cool Mom
- Glen Campbell as Maternity Nurse
- Alice Kernelberg as Roj's Daughter
- Catherine Rose as Caroline's 4-year-old

Reception

Critical reception

Baby Mama received mixed to generally positive reviews from critics. As of February 15, 2009, the review aggregator Rotten Tomatoes reported that 63% of critics gave the film positive reviews based on 153 reviews, with the consensus that the film is "a lightweight, predictable comedy with strong performances." Metacritic reported the film had an average score of 55 out of 100, based on 34 reviews, indicating mixed or average reviews.

Fey and Poehler at the premiere.

In a review for RESOLVE: The National Infertility Association, reproductive lawyer Melissa Brisman comments that this movie should be viewed as entertainment rather than as portraying surrogacy in a factual manner.

Box office

In its opening weekend, *Baby Mama* grossed $17,407,110 in 2,543 theaters in the United States and Canada, ranking #1 at the box office and averaging $6,845 per theater.

Baby Mama grossed a total of $64,163,648, with a production budget of $30 million.

Home media

Baby Mama was released on September 9, 2008 on both DVD and Blu-ray. Extras included commentary with writer/director Michael McCullers and cast members Tina Fey and Amy Poehler, From Conception to Delivery: The Making of Baby Mama Featurette, an alternate ending, deleted scenes, and Saturday Night Live: Legacy of Laughter.

External links

- Official website [1]
- *Baby Mama* [2] at the Internet Movie Database
- *Baby Mama* [3] at Allmovie
- *Baby Mama* [4] at Box Office Mojo
- *Baby Mama* [5] at Rotten Tomatoes
- *Baby Mama* [6] at Metacritic

MacGruber (film)

MacGruber	
Theatrical release poster	
Directed by	Jorma Taccone
Produced by	• Lorne Michaels • John Goldwyn • Ryan Kavanaugh • Seth Meyers • Akiva Schaffer
Written by	• Jorma Taccone • Will Forte • John Solomon
Starring	• Will Forte • Kristen Wiig • Ryan Phillippe • Val Kilmer • Maya Rudolph
Music by	Matthew Compton
Cinematography	Brandon Trost
Editing by	Jamie Gross
Studio	Relativity Media
Distributed by	Rogue Universal Pictures (DVD/Blu-ray only)
Release date(s)	May 21, 2010
Running time	99 minutes
Country	United States
Language	English
Budget	$10 million
Gross revenue	$9,259,314

MacGruber is a 2010 American action comedy film based on the *Saturday Night Live* sketch of the same name, itself a parody of *MacGyver*. The film stars Will Forte in the title role, Kristen Wiig as his love interest/partner, Vicki St. Elmo, Ryan Phillippe as Dixon Piper, a young lieutenant who becomes part of MacGruber's team, Val Kilmer as the aptly named villain, Dieter von Cunth, and Maya Rudolph as the flashbacks and ghost of MacGruber's dead wife, Casey.

The film was released on May 21, 2010, after being pushed from its original April 23 date.

Plot

The film begins in eastern Siberia's Dzhugdzhur Mountains with Dieter Von Cunth (Val Kilmer), the villain, and his men taking control of the X-5 missile, which contains a nuclear warhead. The scene then shifts to an Ecuadorian monastery, where Col. Jim Faith (Powers Boothe) and Lt. Dixon Piper (Ryan Phillippe) have come to find MacGruber. The two military men find MacGruber (Will Forte) meditating in a chapel, and try to convince him to return to the United States. MacGruber refuses, even when he learns that the purpose of his return would be to go after his nemesis, Cunth. However, later that night, MacGruber explodes into a fit of rage after a flashback where Cunth killed his would-be wife Casey Sullivan (Maya Rudolph) at their wedding, and decides to take Faith up on his offer.

MacGruber goes to the Pentagon, and, eventually, finds Col. Faith. After a heated and violent conversation with Faith and Piper, MacGruber decides he will form his own team to pursue Cunth, and will not tolerate Piper on his team. MacGruber visits all his potential team members and is successful in recruiting all but his long time friend Vicki St. Elmo (Kristen Wiig) and Brick Hughes (Big Show), the latter out of homophobia. MacGruber and his team meet Faith and Piper on a tarmac. Upon being questioned where his team is, MacGruber responds that they are in the van (seen in the background) along with his homemade C-4 explosives. The van promptly explodes, killing the whole team. The scene shifts to Faith's office; MacGruber is distraught over the loss of the team and his removal from the Cunth case. In a one on one conversation with Piper, MacGruber repeatedly offers to perform sexual acts on, or with, him if he will join his team. Vicki also arrives, completing MacGruber's team.

The group then travels to Cunth's nightclub in Las Vegas. MacGruber's Miata is insulted by a man driving a car with license plate KFBR392, which he vigorously tries to remember. MacGruber then enters the nightclub and announces who he is and his intentions, as well as where he can be found the next day. The team then tries to set up a sting operation, with Vicki pretending to be MacGruber. However, the van MacGruber and Piper are sitting in is attacked by Haas Bender, one of Cunth's henchmen. MacGruber tells Piper to pass him an Incredi-Mop, which he uses to turn the ignition key and hit the gas pedal, running down Bender. Having Vickie assume the guise of Bender, the team then breaks into a warehouse to stop von Cunth from getting the passcodes to operate the rocket. MacGruber distracts the guards by walking around naked with a piece of celery clenched between his buttocks. Piper manages to kill most of the men inside, but is unable to stop the transfer of the pass codes (due to MacGruber insisting on using a homemade grenade made from a tennis ball, which fizzles). MacGruber and the team then go to a charity event Cunth is holding. MacGruber breaks into a poker game between Cunth and an influential senator. MacGruber tells the senator Cunth is bluffing, which winds up being a very bad move, leading Cunth to win the game. After a heated conversation, MacGruber is thrown out by Cunth's guards who also break Macgruber's beloved stereo, which he eventually does a poor job repairing with duct tape.

After the fiasco, MacGruber returns to the Pentagon where he is told he is a liability. The scene then shifts to MacGruber and Piper drinking and hanging out. However, the two men are suddenly attacked. MacGruber uses Piper as a human shield to survive, and Vicki and MacGruber escape in the Miata. Piper survives due to the fact that he was wearing a bullet proof vest, but is disgusted that MacGruber used him as protection, and leaves him. Vicki and MacGruber then return to Vicki's house where the two have sex. MacGruber then goes to his wife's grave in shame, but he sees her ghost, who gives her blessing to allow MacGruber to pursue Vicki. They have sex immediately afterwards.

Upon returning to Vicki's house (and destroying the car with the license plate KFBR392), MacGruber discovers that Vicki has been kidnapped, and realizes what Cunth's plan is: to bomb the State of the Union address. Cunth calls MacGruber to gloat, but MacGruber is able to trace the call. MacGruber then meets up with Piper to save Vicki. The two men make their way into Cunth's compound, in large part due to MacGruber's propensity for ripping throats. The two are captured and are taken to where Vicki and the missile are located. The group manages to overpower Cunth and his men and handcuff Cunth to a handrail. MacGruber then removes the nuclear component and disables the missile launch before his team escapes as missile explodes. The scene then shifts to MacGruber and Vicki's wedding six months later. Out of the corner of his eye, MacGruber spies a disfigured Cunth (who was believed to have died in the explosion) with an RPG. MacGruber saves Vicki, and then battles Cunth before throwing him off a cliff behind the altar, shooting him with a machine gun as he falls, incinerating the recently dead corpse and finally urinating on it at the foot of the cliff.

Cast

- Will Forte as MacGruber
- Kristen Wiig as Vicki St. Elmo
- Ryan Phillippe as Lt. Dixon Piper
- Val Kilmer as Dieter Von Cunth
- Maya Rudolph as Casey Sullivan
- Powers Boothe as Col. Jim Faith
- Chris Jericho as Frank Korver
- M.V.P. as Vernon Freedom
- The Great Khali as Tug Phelps
- The Big Show as Brick Hughes
- Mark Henry as Tut Beemer
- Kane as Tanker Lutz
- Amar'e Stoudemire as Himself
- Derek Mears as Large Henchman

Production

On the June 1, 2009 episode of *Late Night with Jimmy Fallon* Will Forte announced that *MacGruber* had been greenlit and production was to begin on August 9th, with Fallon adding (in the July 29th episode) that it would be filmed in Albuquerque, New Mexico. Cameos by WWE Superstars Chris Jericho, The Big Show, Mark Henry, Kane, M.V.P. and The Great Khali, and actor Derek Mears, were later confirmed.

Although the film had a release date of May 21, 2010, the film was originally scheduled for an April 23 release.

Legal disputes

Kristen Wiig reprises her role as MacGruber's assistant, Vicki St. Elmo.

Prior to the film's release, *MacGruber* stirred controversy with Lee David Zlotoff, creator of the TV series *MacGyver*, whose contract stipulates he retains the right to a film version of the TV series. His lawyer has sent several cease-and-desist letters and is currently meeting with litigators to determine a course of action. So far no suit has been brought.

Marketing

Pictures were leaked on the Internet on January 6, 2010. A two-minute red band trailer was released on January 19, 2010, and the next day, January 20, a green band trailer was released.

On April 19, 2010, Forte, Wiig, and Phillippe hosted WWE Raw from the Izod Center in East Rutherford, New Jersey in character to promote the film. Forte was also in a handicap match with his "big brother" Khaluber against Vladimir Kozlov, which ended up in Forte winning after Khaluber and Kozlov were counted out.

Ryan Phillippe guest starred on *Saturday Night Live* on April 17, 2010, and made reference to the movie's filming in his opening monologue.

Reception

Critical response

The film has received mixed reviews.

Review aggregator Rotten Tomatoes reports that 47% of all critics have given the film a positive review based on 123 reviews, with an average score of 5.1/10; "top critics," however, scores MacGruber 29% positive, based on 21 reviews, with an average score of 4.4/10. Critics' consensus concludes the movie "too often mistakes shock value for real humor, but MacGruber is better than many SNL films -- and better than it probably should be."

Metacritic, another review aggregator, assigned the film a weighted average score of 43/100 based on 21 reviews from mainstream critics.

Chris Tilly of IGN UK gave the episode 3 out of 5 stars saying "When the film is funny, it's very funny, however, if MacGruber hits as big as he deserves to, we could be seeing a lot more of his mullet on the big-screen in the future."

Jon Peters of KillerFilm gave 3 out of 5 stars saying "It's consistently funny and it didn't need gray tape to do it. It's funny in the old *Airplane!* humor, mixed with a little Mel Brooks, type of way; a rare treat, really." He also added "MacGruber fits nicely somewhere in between *Braddock: Missing in Action III* and *A Man Called Sarge*. But none of this would work, if it wasn't for Will Forte's brilliant blend of witless charm and dumb ass heroics."

Other critics were not nearly as kind, such as Kyle Smith of the New York Post, who called the film "a throbbing flameball of unfunny."

Box office

The film grossed $1.5 million on its opening night, and about $4 million for its opening weekend. The film earned a total of $8,460,995 by the end of its third weekend, still short of the $10 million production cost. In July 2010 *Parade Magazine* listed the film #2 on its list of "Biggest Box Office Flops of 2010 (So Far)."

Theaters typically must exhibit a new release for two weeks before considering dropping it. *MacGruber* realized the fourth biggest third week drop in cinema history, shrinking 93% from 2546 to 177 theaters.

External links

- Official website [1]
- *MacGruber* [2] at the Internet Movie Database
- *MacGruber* [3] at Allmovie
- *MacGruber* [4] at Box Office Mojo
- *MacGruber* [5] at Rotten Tomatoes
- *MacGruber* [6] at Metacritic

A Select Few TV Comedies Produced by Lorne

The Hart and Lorne Terrific Hour

The Hart and Lorne Terrific Hour was a Canadian television variety show, which aired on CBC Television in 1970 and 1971.

The show starred Lorne Michaels and Hart Pomerantz. The cast also included Dan Aykroyd and Victor Garber. The show mixed comedy sketches with musical guests, in a manner similar to *Laugh-In* or Michaels' later *Saturday Night Live*. The show aired on Saturday Nights, following the hugely successful Hockey Night in Canada. Unfortunately, the hockey game would often run over its allotted time, and shorten or completely eliminate the airing of the Terrific Hour.

Sunday Night

Sunday Night / Michelob Presents Night Music	
Format	music variety show
Starring	Jools Holland, David Sanborn, various
Country of origin	United States
No. of episodes	44
Production	
Executive producer(s)	Lorne Michaels
Running time	60 minutes
Broadcast	
Original channel	NBC (season one) syndication (season two)
Original run	1988 – 1990

Sunday Night, later named *Michelob Presents Night Music*, was a late-night television show which aired for two seasons between 1988 and 1990 as a showcase for jazz and electric musical artists. It was hosted by Jools Holland and David Sanborn, and featured Marcus Miller as musical director. Guests included acts such as Sonny Rollins, Shinehead, Sister Carol, Sonic Youth, Joe Sample, Slim Gaillard, Pere Ubu, Pharoah Sanders, and many others. In addition, vintage clips of jazz legends like Thelonious Monk, Dave Brubeck, and Billie Holiday were also featured. The show also featured a house band of Omar Hakim (drums), Marcus Miller (bass), Philippe Saisse (keys), David Sanborn (sax), Hiram Bullock (guitar), and Jools Holland (piano). The show often allowed its guests ample time to explain the origins of their sound, meaning of songs, etc. It also provided a national audience for lesser known acts (like Arto Lindsay's band The Ambitious Lovers). Hal Willner was the music coordinator, responsible for the interesting musical mix-and-matching that took place on the show.

Cast and crew

The Sunday Night Band

plays	1988 1st lineup	1989 2nd lineup	1989 3rd lineup	1989 4th lineup
keys	Philippe Saisse	Philippe Saisse	Philippe Saisse	Philippe Saisse
guitar	Hiram Bullock	Hiram Bullock	Hiram Bullock	Marcus Miller
drums	Omar Hakim	Omar Hakim	Tom Barney	J.T. Lewis
bass	Marcus Miller	Tom Barney	J.T. Lewis	Robben Ford
bass				
drums				
guitar				

Music Associate (keys):	Brenda V. Browne	Brenda V. Browne

Night Music Band

plays	1989 5th lineup		
keys	Philippe Saisse		
guitar	Hiram Bullock		
drums	Omar Hakim		
bass	Tom Barney		
hand drum	Don Alias		

Regular weekly personalities and performers

Hosts:	Jools Holland	(occasional piano or organ accompaniment)
	David Sanborn	(frequent saxophone accompaniment)

Production credits

Title	Name
Sponsor:	Michelob
Production companies:	Broadway Video, Inc. PRA, Inc.
Videotaped at:	Chelsea Television Studios, New York City
Director:	Dave Wilson (1988–1989) John Fortenberry (season 2: 1989 - 1990)

Sunday Night

Musical Directors:	Marcus Miller (1988, 1989)
	George Duke (1989)
	Hiram Bullock (season 2: 1989 - 1990)
	Philippe Saisse (season 2: 1989 - 1990)
Producer:	John Head
Co-Producer:	Patrick Rains

Episodes

Sunday Night musical guest appearances

Show 101	Show 102	Show 103
Ruth Brown	James Taylor	Eddie Palmieri
Ivan Neville	Milton Nascimento	Nelson Gonzales
George Duke	Nana Vasconcelos	Phoebe Snow
	Don Grolnick	Yomo Toro
	Lani Groves	l+
	Dennis Collins	
Show 104	**Show 105**	**Show 106**
Dr. John	Dizzy Gillespie	Slim Gaillard
Mavis Staples	Dianne Reeves	Mark Knopfler
Jeff Healey	David Peaston	Randy Newman
	Onaje Allan Gumbs	Take Six
		l+
Show 107	**Show 108**	**Show 109**
Marianne Faithfull	Jack Bruce	Boz Scaggs
John Zorn	Joe Walsh	Anson Funderburgh
Aaron Neville	Al Green	Betty Wright
Rob Wasserman	Highway 101	Trio Bulgarka
John Sebastian	Nat Hentoff	Dave Bargeron
NRBQ		Randy Brecker
		Ronnie Cuber
		Lou Marini
		l+
Show 110	**Show 111**	**Show 112**

Sunday Night

Al Jarreau Darlene Love Bashiri Johnson Johnny Clegg & Savuka Brenda White Lani Groves Dennis Collins	Earl Klugh Patti Austin Joe Sample Donald Fagen Sister Carol Kasey Cisyk Lani Groves Vaneese Thomas Vivian Cherry Bashiri Johnson	Judy Mowatt Joe Cocker David "Fathead" Newman Ladysmith Black Mambazo Annicia Banks Vaneese Thomas Kasey Cisyk Lani Groves 1+
Show 113	**Show 114**	**Show 115**
Curtis Mayfield Taylor Dayne David Lindley Jorge Cameron Shinehead George Duke	Squeeze Sam Moore Stanley Turrentine Ashford and Simpson Joseph Joubert Steve Thornton George Duke	Youssou N'Dour Theo Diarra Mar Gueye Habib Faye Philip Bailey Lani Groves Marcus Roberts Ambitious Lovers George Duke 1+
Show 116	**Show 117**	**Show 118**
Carlos Santana Lyle Lovett Chester Thompson Armando Peraza José "Chepito" Areas Wayne Shorter Fontella Bass George Duke	Betty Carter Branford Marsalis Willie Dixon John Sebastian George Duke	Take Six Rev. Claude Jeter Rev. Shirley Caesar Ann Caesar Price Bernard Sterling Michael Mathis The Dixie Hummingbirds 1+
Show 119	**Show 120**	**Show 121**
Sonny Rollins Leonard Cohen Ken Nordine Perla Batalla Was (Not Was) Julie Christensen George Duke	Harry Connick, Jr. Lou Reed Gladys Knight John Cale Hiram Bullock Paul Shaffer	Robert Cray John Hiatt Koko Taylor (failed to appear) Tracy Nelson (replacement) World Saxophone Quartet 1+
Show 122	**Compilation 1**	**Compilation 2**

Sunday Night

John Lurie & The Lounge Lizards The Roches Little Milton Campbell Marcus Miller	Yomo Toro (Show 103) Dizzy Gillespie (Show 105) Slim Gaillard (Show 106) Aaron Neville (Show 107) Al Green (Show 108) Boz Scaggs & Betty Wright (Show 109) Savuka (Show 110) Joe Cocker (Show 112) Louis Jordan (archive video)	David Lindley (Show 113) Squeeze (Show 114) Youssous N'Dour (Show 115) Ambitious Lovers (Show 115) Fontella Bass (Show 116) Betty Carter (Show 117) Branford Marsalis (Show 117) Rev. Claude Jeter (Show 118) Leonard Cohen (Show 119) Sonny Rollins (Show 119) Robert Cray & John Hiatt (Show 121)

Night Music musical guest appearances

Show 201	Show 202	Show 203
Stevie Ray Vaughan Pharoah Sanders Van Dyke Parks Maria McKee	Philip Glass Debbie Harry Loudon Wainwright III Pere Ubu	Nona Hendryx Pops Staples Ivo Papasov and his Wedding Band Adrian Belew Elliott Sharp I+
Show 204	**Show 205**	**Show 206**
Bootsy Collins Pretty Fat Carla Bley Steve Swallow Allen Toussaint Karen Mantler & Band	Todd Rundgren Pat Metheny Group Taj Mahal Nanci Griffith Christian Marclay	L.L. Cool J Jean-Luc Ponty Ray Manzarek Elliott Sharp I+
Show 207	**Show 208**	**Show 209**
The Pixies Sun Ra Syd Straw Arthur Baker Al Green Sister Carol	Sting & Fareed Haque Carla Thomas & Rufus Thomas Bill Frisell & Band Mary Margaret O'Hara	Miles Davis Hank Ballard & The Three Midnighters Djavan Marcus Miller Zahar I+
Show 210	**Show 211**	**Show 212**
Sonic Youth Indigo Girls Daniel Lanois Evan Lurie & his Tango Band Diamanda Galás	Eric Clapton Robert Cray Julee Cruise Papa Wemba Dan Hicks & The Acoustic Warriors	Conway Twitty The Residents Kronos Quartet Aster Aweke I+
Show 213	**Show 214**	**Show 215**

Red Hot Chili Peppers Toots Thielemans Charlie Haden & his Liberation Orchestra Nick Cave & Mick Harvey Annabouboula Sister Carol	Graham Parker NRBQ Abbey Lincoln Phil Woods Shabazz and His D.J. C.E. Just Steve Turre and His Sea Shells	Bob Weir Rob Wasserman Warren Zevon Artis the Spoonman John Lurie and Nana Vasconcelos Bongwater Modern Jazz Quartet I+
Show 216	**Show 217**	**Show 218**
Richard Thompson Tim Berne Jo-el Sonnier John Cale & B.J. Cole Shawn Colvin Howard Johnson Sister Carol Hank Crawford	Miles Davis Red Hot Chili Peppers Hank Crawford Abbey Lincoln Kronos Quartet	Eric Clapton and Robert Cray Warren Zevon NRBQ Modern Jazz Quartet Charlie Haden & his Liberation Orchestra Dan Hicks & The Acoustic Warriors Sister Carol Steve Turre and his Sea Shells I+
Compilation 3	**Compilation 4**	
Stevie Ray Vaughan (Show 201) Debbie Harry (Show 202) Al Green (Show 207) The Pixies (Show 207) Miles Davis (Show 209) Eric Clapton and Robert Cray (Show 211)	Pharaoh Sanders (Show 201) Ivo Papasov and his Wedding Band (Show 203) Mary Margaret O'Hara (Show 208) Zahar (Show 209) Abbey Lincoln (Show 214) NRBQ (Show 214) Red Hot Chili Peppers (Show 217)	

External links

- All About Jazz discussion forum [1], with detailed episode listings, as copied from Broadway Video defunct web site listing
- It was the greatest show on television [2], Thus Spake Drake blog, July 23, 2005, with production details, episode listings, and partial song performance listings
- Petition to reissue Night Music (Sunday Night) TV series on DVD or iTunes [3]
- *Sunday Night / Michelob Presents Night Music* [4] at the Internet Movie Database

30 Rock

\	30 Rock
	Title card
Genre	Situation comedy
Created by	Tina Fey
Starring	Tina Fey Jane Krakowski Tracy Morgan Alec Baldwin Jack McBrayer Scott Adsit Judah Friedlander Katrina Bowden Keith Powell Lonny Ross John Lutz Kevin Brown Grizz Chapman Maulik Pancholy
Composer(s)	Jeff Richmond
Country of origin	United States
Language(s)	English
No. of seasons	5
No. of episodes	82 (List of episodes)
Production	
Executive producer(s)	Lorne Michaels Tina Fey Marci Klein David Miner Robert Carlock

Producer(s)	Alec Baldwin Jerry Kupfer Don Scardino
Editor(s)	Ken Eluto, A.C.E.
Location(s)	New York City
Camera setup	Single camera
Running time	21 minutes
Broadcast	
Original channel	NBC
Picture format	HDTV 1080i
Original run	October 11, 2006 – present
External links	
Official website [1]	
Production website [2]	

30 Rock is an American television comedy series created by Tina Fey that airs on NBC. The series is loosely based on Fey's experiences as head writer for Saturday Night Live. *30 Rock* takes place behind the scenes of a fictional live sketch comedy series depicted as airing on NBC; the name "30 Rock" refers to the address of the GE Building where NBC Studios is located, 30 Rockefeller Plaza. This series is produced by Broadway Video and Little Stranger, Inc., in association with NBC Universal.

30 Rock is produced in a single camera setup, and is primarily filmed at Silvercup Studios in Long Island City, Queens, New York, with some scenes filmed on location at Rockefeller Center. The pilot episode premiered on October 11, 2006. Four full seasons have aired since, comprising 21, 15, 22, and 22 episodes respectively. The fourth season began airing on October 15, 2009, and ended on May 20, 2010. The series has an ensemble cast that currently consists of 13 regular cast members, Tina Fey, Tracy Morgan, Jane Krakowski, Jack McBrayer, Scott Adsit, Judah Friedlander, Alec Baldwin, Katrina Bowden, Keith Powell, John Lutz, Kevin Brown, Grizz Chapman and Maulik Pancholy.

30 Rock has been a critical success, winning several major awards (including Emmy Awards for Outstanding Comedy Series in 2007, 2008, and 2009), and achieving the top ranking on myriad critics' year-end best of 2006 and 2007 lists. On July 14, 2009, the series was nominated for 22 Emmy Awards, the most in a single year for a comedy series. Despite these accolades, the series averaged a low 5.8 million viewers in the United States during its first season, according to the Nielsen ratings system, and ranked 102 out of 142 television series. TV commentators have pointed out that *30 Rock* is a low rated show, but it has gained viewers throughout its run. As of March 5, 2010 NBC renewed 30 Rock for a fifth season.

Production

Conception

In 2002, Fey was the head writer and a performer on *Saturday Night Live* (*SNL*). She pitched the show that became *30 Rock* to NBC, originally as a sitcom about cable news. NBC Entertainment president Kevin Reilly felt that "Fey was using the news setting as a fig leaf for her own experience and [he] encouraged her to write what she knew." The show was subsequently reworked to revolve around an *SNL*-style sketch show. In May 2003, Fey signed a contract with NBC to remain in her *SNL* head writer position until at least the 2004–2005 television season and to develop a prime-time project to be produced by Broadway Video and NBC Universal.

During the 2004–2005 pilot season, a pilot was announced named *Untitled Tina Fey Project*. The *30 Rock* pilot focused on the boss of a variety show who has to manage her relationships with the show's volatile star and its charismatic executive producer. The storyline evolved into one that dealt with a head writer of a variety show who dealt with both the stars as well as the show's new network executive. *30 Rock* was officially given the green light to air May 15, 2006, along with a 13-episode order.

The series underwent further changes during the months leading up to and following its debut. A May 2006 press release mentioned that sketches from *The Girlie Show* would be made available in their entirety on NBC's broadband website, DotComedy.com. The idea was to air the fictitious *TGS with Tracy Jordan* online. This aspect of the series was abandoned prior to its debut.

Filming

30 Rock is filmed in New York City. Although establishing shots of *30 Rock* are often repeated, outdoor scenes are filmed on location at Rockefeller Center or in other parts of New York City. Most of the indoor scenes are filmed at Silvercup Studios in Queens. In the episodes "Cleveland" and "Hiatus," Battery Park City, Manhattan, and Douglaston, Queens, doubled for Cleveland, Ohio, and Needmore, Pennsylvania, respectively. In the episode "Gavin Volure," stock footage of the Arkansas Governor's Mansion was used for exterior shots of the home of Steve Martin's character.

The title sequence is made up of photos and video of 30 Rockefeller Plaza and features the series regulars. The sequence ends with a time lapse of the building and then a title card reading '30 Rock'. The sequence has remained mostly the same throughout the series, although there have been changes to the videos of most of the actors.

30 Rock is shot on 35mm film.

Music

The series features a "jaunty" jazz score. Most of the incidental music melody is played by either clarinet, bass clarinet, saxophone, or strings. The music is composed by Fey's husband Jeff Richmond, who is also a producer for *30 Rock*. Richmond wrote the theme music, which was nominated for the Primetime Emmy Award for Outstanding Main Title Theme Music. Seven short, original songs have been featured in episodes, five of which were performed by Jane Krakowski, another performed by Tina Fey and Jason Sudeikis, and another performed by Tracy Morgan. The show has also covered three existing songs, including the song "Midnight Train to Georgia" by Gladys Knight and the Pips. The song had its lyrics altered to accommodate the character Kenneth being "misinformed about the time [of the 11:45 train]." The song "Oh My" performed by The Gray Kid is heard throughout the episode "The Source Awards", which was mixed with a piano arrangement composed by Richmond. "Kidney Now!", a rendition of the popular song, "We Are the World", is performed by various artists in the Season 3 finale. Other popular songs have been featured (with blessings by the singers), like "I Will Remember You" or "Bitch".

Internet content

On April 2, 2008, NBC announced *30 Rock 360*, an online extension of the *30 Rock* series. The extension will feature Jack Donaghy's Online Business Courses (or *Jack U*). Users will also be able to read Jack's blogs and upload their own business advice in video form. Users will be able to submit skits for *TGS with Tracy Jordan* and act out skits from *TGS*. The feature will reopen *Ask Tina*, an interactive question and answer platform in which users can ask Fey questions. Fey will answer the questions in video form. *Ask Tina* was a fixture on NBC.com's *30 Rock* section throughout the first season.

Cast and characters

Main article: Characters of 30 Rock

The plot of *30 Rock* revolves around the cast and crew of the fictional sketch comedy series *TGS with Tracy Jordan* (originally called *The Girlie Show*), which is filmed in Studio 6H inside 30 Rockefeller Plaza. The series features an ensemble cast. The series features seven roles that receive star billing during the opening credits:

- Tina Fey as Liz Lemon, the protagonist of the series and head writer of *TGS with Tracy Jordan*.
- Jane Krakowski as Jenna Maroney, Original star of "The Girlie Show", limelight-seeking co-star of *TGS* and Liz's best friend.
- Tracy Morgan as Tracy Jordan, loose cannon, crazy, unpredictable star of *TGS*.
- Jack McBrayer as Kenneth Parcell, a cheerful, obedient Southern-born NBC page, who "lives for television."

- Scott Adsit as Pete Hornberger, the "sane," quick-witted producer of *TGS*, who serves as Liz's most trusted friend.
- Judah Friedlander as Frank Rossitano, a trucker hat-wearing, childish, sarcastic writer at *TGS*. His hat bears a different phrase in every episode.
- Alec Baldwin as Jack Donaghy, the decisive, controlling, suave and occasionally senseless network executive who constantly interferes with the goings-on at *TGS*.

Beginning with season two, three characters, who were credited as guest stars during season one, received star billing after the opening credits in addition to the principal cast:

- Katrina Bowden as Cerie Xerox, Liz's attractive, laid-back assistant, who usually wears revealing outfits to work, much to the delight of the writer's room.
- Keith Powell as James "Toofer" Spurlock, the proud African-American Harvard University alumnus writer, who often butts heads with Tracy and Frank.
- Lonny Ross as Josh Girard, a young and immature *TGS* writer and co-star, known for his impressions. Ross was written out in season four.

Beginning with season three, three characters who were credited as guest stars in the first two seasons received star billing after the opening credits in addition to Bowden, Powell, Ross, and the principal cast. They are credited only in the episodes in which they appear:

- Kevin Brown as Dot Com, an erudite member of Tracy's entourage, he is also a Wesleyan University-trained stage actor. His real name is Walter Slattery.
- Grizz Chapman as Grizz, a member of Tracy's entourage.
- Maulik Pancholy as Jonathan, Jack's loyal and overprotective personal assistant, who at times appears to be possibly in love with Jack.

Beginning with season four, episode seven, one character who was credited as a guest star in the first three seasons received star billing after the opening credits in addition to Bowden, Powell, Brown, Chapman, and Pancholy:

- John Lutz as J.D. Lutz, an Oberlin-educated member of the writing staff.

Casting

Tina Fey worked with Jen McNamara and Adam Bernstein for the casting of the series. Fey's first act as casting director was to cast herself as the lead character, Liz Lemon, who is said to be much like Fey herself when she first became head writer on *SNL*. The next actor to be cast was Tracy Morgan as Tracy Jordan, who was then a former castmate of Fey's in *SNL*. Morgan was asked by Fey to play the role, and he believed it was "right up [his] alley and it was tailor made for [him]". Fey said that the character of Kenneth Parcell was written with Jack McBrayer in mind. McBrayer is an old friend of Fey (they worked together at Second City in Chicago), and she "really wanted him for that part and was very happy when no one objected".

Rachel Dratch, Fey's longtime comedy partner and fellow *SNL* alumna, was originally cast to portray Jenna. Dratch played the role in the show's original pilot, but in August 2006, Jane Krakowski was announced as Dratch's replacement, with Dratch remaining involved in the show playing various characters. Fey explained the change by noting that Dratch was "better-suited to playing a variety of eccentric side characters", and that the role of Jenna was more of a straight-ahead acting part. Although Fey went on to say that "Rachel and I were both very excited about this new direction", Dratch said that she was not happy with the media's depiction of the change as a demotion. Dratch was skeptical about the reasons she was given for the change, and was not happy with the reduction in the number of episodes in which she would appear.

Shortly following the casting of McBrayer and Dratch, Alec Baldwin was cast as Jack Donaghy, the "totally uncensored" Vice President of East Coast Television and Microwave Oven Programming. Fey said that the character of Jack Donaghy was written with Baldwin in mind, and she was "very pleasantly surprised when he agreed to do it". Judah Friedlander was cast as Frank Rossitano, a staff writer of *The Girlie Show*. Friedlander had never met Fey before auditioning for a role in *30 Rock*. His character was based on at least two writers that Fey used to work with at *SNL*, but he has said that he "certainly brought some of [his] own things to it as well". Finally, Scott Adsit was cast as Pete Hornberger, a long time friend of Liz's and producer of *The Girlie Show*. Adsit, an old friend of Fey, also had his character written based on him.

Season synopses

See also: List of 30 Rock episodes

Season 1

Main article: 30 Rock (season 1)

Season one began airing in the United States on October 11, 2006, and featured 21 episodes. The season finale aired on April 26, 2007. Jack Donaghy, the "Head of East Coast Television and Microwave Oven Programming" at General Electric (GE), is transferred to work at the NBC headquarters, 30 Rockefeller Plaza, and retool the late night sketch comedy series *The Girlie Show*. The show's cast and crew are outraged by this; especially head writer Liz Lemon and main actress Jenna Maroney. Jack proceeds to wreak havoc on *The Girlie Show,* forcing Liz to hire the off-the-wall movie star Tracy Jordan. He again angers the cast and crew of *The Girlie Show* when he changes the name to *TGS with Tracy Jordan* (or just *TGS*).

As the season progresses, the episodes become less about *TGS* and more about how the characters deal with juggling their lives and their jobs — specifically the protagonist, Liz Lemon, but other characters are also explored. Episodes also become less self-contained and various story arcs develop in the second half of the season. For example, the first major story arc centers on Liz's relationship with Dennis Duffy (Dean Winters), "The Beeper King." Other story arcs include: Jenna promoting her movie *The Rural Juror*; Tracy going on the run from the Black Crusaders; Jack's engagement, which was eventually called off, to a Christie's auctioneer named Phoebe (Emily Mortimer); and another relationship of Liz's with Floyd (Jason Sudeikis).

Guest stars include Isabella Rossellini, Emily Mortimer, Will Arnett, Elaine Stritch, Whoopi Goldberg, and Conan O'Brien.

Season 2

Main article: 30 Rock (season 2)

Season two began airing in the United States on October 4, 2007, and featured 15 episodes. The second season was originally intended to consist of 22 episodes but the order was cut to 15 due to the 2007–2008 Writers Guild of America strike. The season finale aired on May 8, 2008. After Liz broke up with Floyd in the summer, she is looking for ways to rebound. When Jerry Seinfeld confronts Jack about a new marketing campaign which featured clips of Seinfeld's sitcom, *Seinfeld*, in all NBC shows, he has a chance encounter with Liz that gives her some much needed advice. During the *TGS* summer hiatus, Jenna becomes overweight due to performing in the Broadway show *Mystic Pizza: The Musical* (based on the real 1988 film *Mystic Pizza*) and with the help of Kenneth, loses the weight. Tracy has encountered some marital problems with his wife Angie Jordan (Sherri Shepherd) and they become separated, but later reunite.

During the season, Jack develops a relationship with a Democratic congresswoman named Celeste "C.C." Cunningham (Edie Falco). They later break up. An arc that was established in the first season but becomes more apparent in the second regards Jack running for the GE chairmanship against his archnemesis Devon Banks (Will Arnett). The season ends with Liz planning to adopt a child after believing she was pregnant with Dennis' baby. Kenneth also travels to Beijing to be a page at the 2008 Summer Olympics and Tracy invents a pornographic video game. Jack ends the season working at a new government job in Washington, D.C., but plans to get fired by proposing a "gay bomb."

Season 3

Main article: 30 Rock (season 3)

30 Rock returned with a third season as part of NBC's fall schedule, airing immediately after *The Office*. The season consisted of 22 episodes. Oprah Winfrey guest starred in the second episode, playing herself, as well as Jennifer Aniston playing Liz's ex roommate. Salma Hayek also appeared for a multi-episode arc, portraying Jack's new girlfriend, Elisa. Other guest stars this season included John Lithgow, Megan Mullally and Steve Martin. Jon Hamm played Liz's love interest and neighbor for several episodes. Alan Alda appeared in the season's final two episodes as Milton Greene, Jack's biological father. The season finale featured multiple musical guests, including Talib Kweli, Michael McDonald, Norah Jones, Steve Earle, Clay Aiken, the Beastie Boys, Mary J. Blige, Elvis Costello, Sheryl Crow, Rhett Miller, Cyndi Lauper, Adam Levine, Sara Bareilles, Wyclef Jean, and Rachael Yamagata, performing "Kidney Now!", an organ donation drive spoof of *We Are The World* and "Just Stand Up!".

Salma Hayek appeared in six episodes as Elisa, Jack's girlfriend and his mother's nurse.

Season 4

Main article: 30 Rock (season 4)

The fourth season of *30 Rock* premiered on October 15, 2009. Like the previous season 3, it also consisted of 22 episodes. A recurring story arc early in the season revolved around Jack's request that Liz cast a new actor for *TGS*, and Liz's subsequent search for the perfect comedian, much to the dismay of Jenna and Tracy, who fear losing their spotlight. The later half of the season focused on two complementary story arcs: Jack's inability to choose between two mistresses, and Liz's inability to find a boyfriend to live up to her expectations. The season has also featured such guest stars as Julianne Moore, Jon Bon Jovi, Elizabeth Banks, Michael Sheen, Matt Damon, Will Ferrell, and James Franco.

Season 5

Main article: 30 Rock (season 5)

On March 5, 2010, NBC announced *30 Rock* had been renewed for a fifth season, which is set to air in the 2010–2011 TV season. The season airs on the Thursday 8:30 p.m. time slot and premiered on September 23.

On July 31, 2010, NBC announced that an episode of *30 Rock*'s fifth season would be filmed and broadcast live, twice, on the evening of October 14, 2010. The two separate recordings will result in a live telecast of the episode to American viewers in both the West and East Coast.

Effect

Critical reception

30 Rock has been well received by critics but has struggled to attract viewers. Robert Abele of *LA Weekly* declared that the show was "A weirdly appropriate and hilarious symbol of our times." *The Wall Street Journal*'s Dorothy Rabinowitz wrote that "The standard caution is relevant – debut episodes tend to be highly polished. All the more reason to enjoy the hilarious scenes and fine ensemble cast here." Some less favorable reviews were received from Brian Lowry of *Variety*. Lowry said that "Despite her success with 'Mean Girls,' [Tina] Fey mostly hits too-familiar notes in the pilot. Moreover, she's a limited protagonist, which is problematic." Criticism was also received from Maureen Ryan of the *Chicago Tribune*, who said that "*30 Rock* is less than the sum of its parts, and, as an entry in the single-camera comedy sweepstakes, it fails to show either the inspired inventiveness of *Arrested Development* or provide the surprisingly perceptive character studies of *The Office*." Metacritic gave the pilot episode a Metascore—a weighted average based on the impressions of a select thirty-one critical reviews—of 67 out of 100.

At the end of 2006, *LA Weekly* listed *30 Rock* as one of the best "Series of the Year." The show also appeared on similar year end "best of" 2006 lists published by *The New York Times*, *The A.V. Club*, *The Boston Globe*, *The Chicago Sun-Times*, *Entertainment Weekly*, *The Los Angeles Times*, *The Miami Herald*, *People Weekly*, and *TV Guide*. The *Associated Press* wrote that NBC's "Thursday night comedy block—made up of *My Name Is Earl*, *The Office*, *Scrubs*, and *30 Rock*—is consistently the best night of prime time viewing for any network." In 2007, it appeared on *The Boston Globe*'s "best of" list as well as the "best of" lists of *The Chicago Sun-Times*, *The Chicago Tribune*, *Entertainment Weekly*, *The Los Angeles Times*, *Newark Star-Ledger*, *The New York Times*, *Pittsburgh Post-Gazette*, *The San Francisco Chronicle*, *The San Jose Mercury News*, *TV Guide* and *USA Today*. *30 Rock* was named the best series of 2007 by *Entertainment Weekly*.

In December 2009, *Newsweek* magazine ranked *30 Rock* as the best comedy on TV for the past decade, 2000–2010.

Awards and nominations

Main article: List of 30 Rock awards and nominations

Capping its critically successful first season, *30 Rock* won the Primetime Emmy Award for Outstanding Comedy Series and Elaine Stritch was awarded an Emmy in September 2007 for her work as a guest actress in "Hiatus." Tina Fey and Alec Baldwin were nominated in the Outstanding Lead Actress and Outstanding Lead Actor in a comedy series categories respectively. "Jack-Tor" and "Tracy Does Conan" were both nominated in the category of Outstanding Writing for a Comedy Series. *30 Rock* received four Creative Arts Emmy Awards. Alec Baldwin received the Golden Globe Award for Best Performance by an Actor in a Television Series – Comedy or Musical in 2007. Baldwin also received the Screen Actors Guild Award for Outstanding Performance by a Male Actor in a Comedy Series in 2007. The show also received various other guild award nominations during its first season.

In 2008, Tina Fey and Alec Baldwin both won Screen Actors Guild Awards. The series took home the Writers Guild of America Award for Best Comedy Series in 2008. It also received the Danny Thomas Producer of the Year Award in Episodic Series – Comedy from the Producers Guild of America in 2008. *30 Rock* received 17 Emmy nominations, for its second season, meaning it was the second most nominated series of the year. These 17 nominations broke the record for the most nominations for a comedy series, meaning that *30 Rock* was the most nominated comedy series for any individual Emmy year. The previous holder of this record was *The Larry Sanders Show* in 1996 with 16 nominations. *30 Rock* also won the Television Critics Association Award for "Outstanding Achievement in Comedy."

Also in 2008, *30 Rock* completed a sweep of the major awards for best comedy series at that year's Primetime Emmy Awards. The show won Outstanding Comedy Series, Alec Baldwin was recognized as Outstanding Lead Actor in a Comedy Series, and Tina Fey was given the award for Outstanding Lead Actress in a Comedy Series. This marks the eighth time in the history of the Emmy awards that a show won best series plus best lead actor and actress. Tina Fey also won the award for Outstanding Writing in a Comedy Series for the episode "Cooter".

At the 2008 Golden Globe awards, *30 Rock* won the award for Best Television Series – Musical or Comedy, Alec Baldwin won Best Actor in a Television Musical or Comedy, and Tina Fey won Best Actress in a Television Musical or Comedy.

30 Rock received a Peabody Award in 2008. Upon announcing the award, the Peabody Board commended the show for being "not only a great workplace comedy in the tradition of *The Mary Tyler Moore Show*, complete with fresh, indelible secondary characters, but also a sly, gleeful satire of corporate media, especially the network that airs it."

In 2009, 30 Rock received a record breaking 22 primetime Emmy Award nominations and won 5 Emmy Awards, including Best Comedy Series and Best Actor in a Comedy Series (Alec Baldwin).

Ratings

Below, "Rank" refers to how well *30 Rock* rated compared to other television series which aired during primetime hours of the corresponding television season. The television season tends to begin in September, of any given year, and end during the May of the following year. "Viewers" refers to the average number of viewers for all original episodes (broadcast in the series' "Regular Timeslot") of *30 Rock* aired during the television season. Although the viewer average may be higher for some seasons than others, the rank will not necessarily be higher. This is due to the number of programs aired during primetime. In some seasons there may be more regular programs aired during primetime than in others. The "Season premiere" is the date that the first episode of the season aired. Similarly, the "Season finale" is the date that the final episode of the season aired.

Season	Timeslot (EST)	Episodes	Season premiere	Season finale	TV season	Rank	Viewers (in millions)
1	Wednesday 8:00 P.M. (October 11, 2006 – November 1, 2006) Thursday 9:30 P.M. (November 16, 2006 – March 8, 2007) Thursday 9:00 P.M. (April 5, 2007 – April 26, 2007)	21	October 11, 2006	April 26, 2007	2006–2007	#102	5.8
2	Thursday 8:30 P.M. (October 4, 2007 – December 6, 2007) Thursday 9:00 P.M. (December 13, 2007) Thursday 8:30 P.M. (January 10, 2008 – April 17, 2008) Thursday 9:30 P.M. (April 24, 2008 – May 8, 2008)	15	October 4, 2007	May 8, 2008	2007–2008	#94	6.4
3	Thursday 9:30 P.M. (October 30, 2008 – May 14, 2009)	22	October 30, 2008	May 14, 2009	2008–2009	#69	7.5
4	Thursday 9:30 P.M. (October 15, 2009 – May 20, 2010) Thursday 9:00 P.M. (January 14, 2010) Thursday 8:30 P.M. (April 22, 2010)	22	October 15, 2009	May 20, 2010	2009–2010	#86	5.9
5	Thursday 8:30 P.M. (September 23, 2010 – TBA)	22	September 23, 2010	TBA	2010–2011	TBA	5.7 (to date)

* As of the latest episode in the season.

The pilot episode generated 8.13 million viewers, the series' highest ratings until that of its third season premiere which garnered 8.5 million viewers. In its original timeslot of Wednesday at 8:00PM EST, the show averaged 6.23 million viewers. *30 Rock* aired on Wednesdays for its first four episodes. The season's lowest ratings were achieved by "Jack the Writer" and "Hard Ball" which both achieved 4.61 million viewers. The season two premiere, "SeinfeldVision," was viewed by 7.33 million viewers, the highest rating since the pilot. *30 Rock* entered a hiatus due to the 2007–2008 Writers Guild of America strike on January 10, 2008. The episode that aired on that date was viewed by 5.98 million viewers. The second season finale, "Cooter", which aired on May 8, 2008, was viewed by 5.6 million viewers.

On December 29, 2006, Nielsen Media Research (NMR) reported the results of having, for the first time, monitored viewers who use a digital video recorder to record shows for later viewing. NMR reported that *30 Rock* adds nearly 7.5% to its total audience every week as a result of viewers who use a DVR to record the show and then watch it within a week of its initial airing. A March 2007 report from *MAGNA Global*, based on NMR data about viewership ranked by among adults 25–54, shows that as of the time of the report *30 Rock*'s viewers have a median income of $65,000, high enough to place the show tied at 11th in affluence with several other shows. This is during a period where for the season *30 Rock* is tied at No. 85 in the 18–49 demographic. During its second season, *30 Rock* ranked in fourth place, against all primetime programming, for television series' which are watched by viewers with income above $100,000. Following Fey's popular impressions of Alaskan governor Sarah Palin on *Saturday Night Live*, the third season premiere was seen by 8.5 million viewers, making it the highest viewed episode in the series. The premiere earned a 4.1 preliminary adults 18–49 rating, an increase of 21% from the second season premiere.

In other countries

30 Rock also airs in other countries; ratings and rankings for some of these markets include:

- Latin America: Seasons 1, 2, 3 and 4 have aired on Sony Entertainment Television, a cable network in the Latin American market which shows a number of U.S. prime time programs from NBC, CBS, ABC and the Lifetime network, as well as syndicated U.S. series.
- Canada: The series premiered on the CTV network on October 10, 2006, a day before its premiere in the United States. The network aired the first four episodes of the series, but dropped the show effective November 30, 2006 after a brief run during which it never entered the Bureau of Broadcast Measurement Nielsen top 30. CTV later re-added the show to its lineup on Sundays at 8:30pm, but moved the show to its secondary A-Channel system for the series' second season. From the third season onward, it has aired on Citytv.
- United Kingdom: The first season premiered on October 11, 2007 on Five. The premiere was watched by 700,000 viewers, which was 6% of all people watching television in the country at the time it was broadcast. *30 Rock* originally aired at 10:45pm, but was moved to 11:05pm, airing back-to-back episodes. Season two was broadcast from February 20, 2009 at 9pm on Five USA. Season 3 began airing on UK digital TV station Comedy Central, starting Monday October 5, 2009. Comedy Central began airing double episodes of Season 4 on Monday evenings at 22.00 from 19 April 2010.
- South Africa: All three seasons have been aired on M-Net, the 4th season will be aired soon.
- Ireland: Seasons 1, 2, 4 have shown on 3e
- Germany: ZDFneo, a new digital channel from ZDF, was launched on November 1, 2009, with the German-dubbed version of *30 Rock* as its flagship program. The series' free television debut that night on that channel registered a 0.0 rating, with fewer than 5000 viewers tuning in. TNT Serie, a German version of the TNT channel, broadcast the series to cable and pay satellite viewers since February 2009.
- Greece: 30 Rock originally airs on Universal Channel Greece. The first season of the series finished airing on Alter Channel in July 2010.

- Portugal: The first two seasons have aired on FOX:Next which is currently airing Season 3.
- Slovenia: Season 1 came to POP TV on 12 April 2010 (airing from Monday to Thursday). It concluded on 17 May 2010.
- Croatia: Nova TV aired Seasons 1 and 2, currently airing Season 3 (always at Sunday midnight time slot).
- India: Star World has aired the three seasons over the years and aired the 4th Season in 2010 (11:00pm).
- Hong Kong: ATV World has aired Seasons 1-3 from July 2010 to Oct 2010 (Mon-Tue, Thu-Fri 8:30pm)

Australian ratings

- Australia: The first season premiered on December 4, 2007 on the Seven Network at 22.30, showing on Mondays and Wednesdays. After the summer season its timeslot was changed to Mondays only, showing at 23.30. The first season completed its run on April 28, 2008, and the DVD was released two days later. The second season premiered on June 9, 2008 at 23.30. The third season began airing on February 2, 2009, returning at 23.30 on Mondays.

The Seven Network returned the show in December 2009 at the earlier time of 22.30 Mondays and Tuesdays, repeating season 3 in preparation for season 4. Oddly, viewers grew from word of mouth and its general non-TV-broadcast popularity, and ratings even doubled from recent years. Despite this unexpected surge, the network has decided to return the show to the graveyard time-slot of 23.30 Mondays for season four, of which the first episode aired on the 1st of February, 2010. It is now being shown on the new high-definition digital channel 7mate on Mondays at the more accessible timeslot of 21:30.

# Series	# Episode	Episode	AU Air Date	Timeslot	Viewers
Season 3					
37	1	"Do-Over"	February 2, 2009	11:30 P.M.	281,000
38	2	"Believe in the Stars"	February 16, 2009	11:20 P.M.	306,000
39	3	"The One with the Cast of *Night Court*"	February 23, 2009	11:30 P.M.	228,000
40	4	"Gavin Volure"	March 2, 2009	11:20 P.M.	273,000
41	5	"Reunion"	March 9, 2009	11:20 P.M.	292,000

42	6	"Christmas Special"	March 16, 2009	11:20 P.M.	230,000
43	7	"Señor Macho Solo"	March 23, 2009	11:20 P.M.	296,000
44	8	"Flu Shot"	March 30, 2009	11:20 P.M.	245,000
45	9	"Retreat to Move Forward"	April 6, 2009	11:40 P.M.	233,000
46	10	"Generalissimo"	April 13, 2009	11:40 P.M.	265,000
47	11	"St. Valentine's Day"	April 20, 2009	11:20 P.M.	294,000
48	12	"Larry King"	April 27, 2009	11:20 P.M.	267,000
49	13	"Goodbye, My Friend"	May 4, 2009	11:20 P.M.	282,000
50	14	"The Funcooker"	May 18, 2009	11:25 P.M.	200,000
51	15	"The Bubble"	May 25, 2009	11:45 P.M.	205,000
52	16	"Apollo, Apollo"	June 1, 2009	11:30 P.M.	180,000
53	17	"Cutbacks"	June 8, 2009	11:25 P.M.	196,000
54	18	"Jackie Jormp-Jomp"	June 15, 2009	11:30 P.M.	224,000
55	19	"The Ones"	June 22, 2009	11:20 P.M.	248,000
56	20	"The Natural Order"	June 29, 2009	11:35 P.M.	194,000
57	21	"Mamma Mia"	July 6, 2009	11:30 P.M.	186,000

Similarities to other media

Two shows debuting on 2006–07 NBC lineup, *30 Rock* and *Studio 60 on the Sunset Strip*, revolved around the off-camera happenings on a sketch comedy series. Similarities between the two led to speculation that only one of them would be picked up. Baldwin said "I'd be stunned if NBC picked up both shows. And ours has the tougher task, as a comedy, because if it's not funny, that's it." Kevin Reilly, then president of NBC Entertainment, was supportive of Fey, describing the situation as a "high-class problem":

> I just can't imagine the audience would look at both shows, choose one and cancel the other out. In some ways, why is it any different than when there have been three or four cop shows on any schedule, or *Scrubs* and *ER*, which are totally very different?

Evidence of the overlapping subject matter between the shows, as well as the conflict between them, arose when Aaron Sorkin, the creator of *Studio 60 on the Sunset Strip*, asked Lorne Michaels to allow him to observe *Saturday Night Live* for a week, a request Michaels denied. Despite this, Sorkin sent Fey flowers after NBC announced it would pick up both series, and wished her luck with *30 Rock*. Fey said that "it's just bad luck for me that in my first attempt at prime time I'm going up against the most powerful writer on television. I was joking that this would be the best pilot ever aired on Trio. And then Trio got canceled." Fey wound up "beating" Sorkin when *Studio 60* was canceled after one season and *30 Rock* was renewed for a second. Though *30 Rock*'s first-season ratings proved lackluster and were lower than those of *Studio 60*, *Studio 60* was more expensive to produce.

One early promo for *30 Rock* portrayed Alec Baldwin mistakenly thinking he would meet Sorkin, and when asked on her "Ask Tina" space what she thought of the criticism that *30 Rock* received, Fey jokingly replied that people who did not like it were probably confusing it with *Studio 60*. However, none of *30 Rocks* producers have given *Studio 60* any serious criticism, positive or negative. In a November 1, 2006 interview, Fey said she had seen the first two episodes of *Studio 60*. When asked what her impressions were, she jokingly replied, "I can't do impressions of Bradley Whitford and Matthew Perry."

At least four *30 Rock* episodes have briefly parodied *Studio 60*:

- "Jack the Writer" contains a self-referring walk and talk sequence, such sequences being commonly used on *Studio 60* and Aaron Sorkin's previous shows.
- "Jack-tor" – Liz tries to quote global education statistics, only to mess up and realize that she does not know what she is talking about.
- "Jack Meets Dennis" – Liz says the upcoming show will be "worse than that time we did that Gilbert and Sullivan parody". The second episode of *Studio 60*, "The Cold Open," included a parody of the "Major-General's Song" on the show-within-the-show.
- "The Fabian Strategy" - In the ending sequence Kenneth watches the credits for TGS, which include Ricky and Ronnie as writers, the two ex-head writers on *Studio 60*.

Some critics have compared *30 Rock* to *The Mary Tyler Moore Show*, with parallels drawn between the relationship of Liz and Jack and that of Mary Richards and Lou Grant. It has also been compared to *That Girl*. Like *That Girl* and *Mary Tyler Moore*, *30 Rock* is a sitcom centering on an unmarried, brunette career woman living in a big city where she works in the television industry. "That Girl" was parodied in the opening segment of 30 Rock's pilot.

Internet and DVD

Episode downloads and online streaming

Weekly installments of *30 Rock* are available to download for a per-episode fee, to U.S. residents only, via the "NBC Direct" service, Amazon Unbox and Apple's iTunes Store. In addition to paid downloads, the first four seasons can be streamed on Netflix, but this requires a paid subscription. Both NBC.com and Hulu.com stream episodes for free, but only the five most current installments are available for viewing.

DVD releases

Name	Region 1	Region 2	Region 4	Discs	Extras
Season One	September 4, 2007	March 17, 2008	April 30, 2008	3	Episode commentaries, Outtakes and Deleted scenes.
Season Two	October 7, 2008	May 25, 2009	January 8, 2009	2	Episode commentaries, Outtakes, Deleted scenes, The table read for the episode "Cooter," *30 Rock* Live at the UCB Theatre, a behind-the-scenes look at an episode of *Saturday Night Live* which was hosted by Tina Fey, and The Academy of Television Arts & Sciences Presents: An Evening With *30 Rock*.
Season Three	September 22, 2009	April 5, 2010	November 11, 2009	3	Episode commentaries, Outtakes, Deleted scenes, The table read for the episode "Kidney Now!", behind-the-scenes with the Muppets, 1-900-OKFACE, The Making of "He Needs a Kidney", Photo Gallery.
Season Four	September 21, 2010	February 21, 2011	November 3, 2010	3	Episode commentaries, Deleted scenes, Behind-the-scenes, Extended episodes, *Ace of Cakes* episode, "Tennis Night in America" music video, Photo Gallery.

External links

- Official website [1]
- *30 Rock* [3] at TV Guide
- *30 Rock* [4] at the Internet Movie Database
- *30 Rock* [5] at TV.com
- 30 Rock [6] at Comedy Central UK
- 30 Rock [7] at 30Rock Quotes.net

Article Sources and Contributors

Lorne Michaels *Source*: http://en.wikipedia.org/?oldid=389984785 *Contributors*: Murtaugh.mk

Rowan & Martin's Laugh-In *Source*: http://en.wikipedia.org/?oldid=390439787 *Contributors*: Blaine Washington

Saturday Night Live *Source*: http://en.wikipedia.org/?oldid=390223385 *Contributors*: 1 anonymous edits

Broadway Video *Source*: http://en.wikipedia.org/?oldid=388353264 *Contributors*: 1 anonymous edits

Three Amigos *Source*: http://en.wikipedia.org/?oldid=389957647 *Contributors*: AbsoluteGleek92

Coneheads (film) *Source*: http://en.wikipedia.org/?oldid=389172946 *Contributors*: 1 anonymous edits

Wayne's World (film) *Source*: http://en.wikipedia.org/?oldid=390238724 *Contributors*: 1 anonymous edits

Tommy Boy *Source*: http://en.wikipedia.org/?oldid=388501007 *Contributors*: 1 anonymous edits

Brain Candy *Source*: http://en.wikipedia.org/?oldid=379544773 *Contributors*: Sreejithk2000

A Night at the Roxbury *Source*: http://en.wikipedia.org/?oldid=386435625 *Contributors*: RepublicanJacobite

Mean Girls *Source*: http://en.wikipedia.org/?oldid=390191073 *Contributors*: Hmrox

Baby Mama (film) *Source*: http://en.wikipedia.org/?oldid=390089621 *Contributors*: 1 anonymous edits

MacGruber (film) *Source*: http://en.wikipedia.org/?oldid=389874893 *Contributors*: Donaldo1997

The Hart and Lorne Terrific Hour *Source*: http://en.wikipedia.org/?oldid=332046832 *Contributors*:

Sunday Night *Source*: http://en.wikipedia.org/?oldid=377611040 *Contributors*: Tassedethe

30 Rock *Source*: http://en.wikipedia.org/?oldid=390032907 *Contributors*: 1 anonymous edits

Image Sources, Licenses and Contributors

Image:Lorne Michaels David Shankbone 2010.jpg *Source*: http://bibliocm.bibliolabs.com/mwAnon/index.php?title=File:Lorne_Michaels_David_Shankbone_2010.jpg *License*: Creative Commons Attribution 3.0 *Contributors*: David Shankbone

File:Lorne Michaels at the 2008 Tribeca Film Festival.JPG *Source*: http://bibliocm.bibliolabs.com/mwAnon/index.php?title=File:Lorne_Michaels_at_the_2008_Tribeca_Film_Festival.JPG *License*: Creative Commons Attribution 3.0 *Contributors*: David Shankbone

Image:Lorne Michaels by David Shankbone.jpg *Source*: http://bibliocm.bibliolabs.com/mwAnon/index.php?title=File:Lorne_Michaels_by_David_Shankbone.jpg *License*: GNU Free Documentation License *Contributors*: David Shankbone

File:29 - New York - Octobre 2008.jpg *Source*: http://bibliocm.bibliolabs.com/mwAnon/index.php?title=File:29_-_New_York_-_Octobre_2008.jpg *License*: Creative Commons Attribution-Sharealike 3.0 *Contributors*: User:S23678

File:SNL stage.jpg *Source*: http://bibliocm.bibliolabs.com/mwAnon/index.php?title=File:SNL_stage.jpg *License*: Creative Commons Attribution 2.0 *Contributors*: Rex Sorgatz from New York

Image:Brillbuilding2009.jpg *Source*: http://bibliocm.bibliolabs.com/mwAnon/index.php?title=File:Brillbuilding2009.jpg *License*: Creative Commons Attribution-Sharealike 3.0 *Contributors*: NYCfoto

File:Flag of the United States.svg *Source*: http://bibliocm.bibliolabs.com/mwAnon/index.php?title=File:Flag_of_the_United_States.svg *License*: Public Domain *Contributors*: User:Dbenbenn, User:Indolences, User:Jacobolus, User:Technion, User:Zscout370

File:WaynesWorldAMCPacer.jpg *Source*: http://bibliocm.bibliolabs.com/mwAnon/index.php?title=File:WaynesWorldAMCPacer.jpg *License*: Creative Commons Attribution 2.0 *Contributors*: dave_7

File:Star full.svg *Source*: http://bibliocm.bibliolabs.com/mwAnon/index.php?title=File:Star_full.svg *License*: Public Domain *Contributors*: User:Conti, User:RedHotHeat

File:Star empty.svg *Source*: http://bibliocm.bibliolabs.com/mwAnon/index.php?title=File:Star_empty.svg *License*: Creative Commons Attribution-Sharealike 2.5 *Contributors*: User:Conti, User:RedHotHeat

File:Star half.svg *Source*: http://bibliocm.bibliolabs.com/mwAnon/index.php?title=File:Star_half.svg *License*: Creative Commons Attribution-Sharealike 2.5 *Contributors*: User:Conti

Image:Amy Poehler and Tina Fey by David Shankbone.jpg *Source*: http://bibliocm.bibliolabs.com/mwAnon/index.php?title=File:Amy_Poehler_and_Tina_Fey_by_David_Shankbone.jpg *License*: GNU Free Documentation License *Contributors*: David Shankbone

File:KristenWiigTime100May08.jpg *Source*: http://bibliocm.bibliolabs.com/mwAnon/index.php?title=File:KristenWiigTime100May08.jpg *License*: Attribution *Contributors*: Rachel Sklar at http://www.flickr.com/photos/rachelsklar/

File:30Rock logo.svg *Source*: http://bibliocm.bibliolabs.com/mwAnon/index.php?title=File:30Rock_logo.svg *License*: unknown *Contributors*: 30_rock_logo.png: w:en:30 Rock30 Rock derivative work: Mattbiemer

File:Salma Hayek Cannes 2010.jpg *Source*: http://bibliocm.bibliolabs.com/mwAnon/index.php?title=File:Salma_Hayek_Cannes_2010.jpg *License*: Creative Commons Attribution-Sharealike 3.0 *Contributors*: Georges Biard

The cover image herein is used under a Creative Commons License and may be reused or reproduced under that same license.

http://upload.wikimedia.org/wikipedia/commons/3/36/Lorne_Michaels_by_David_Shankbone.jpg

CPSIA information can be obtained at www.ICGtesting.com
Printed in the USA
LVOW040147201011
251308LV00002B/286/P